Ruined

"Set apart. Living fearless. Being dangerous!"

CHRIS ESTRADA

Published by:
R.H. Publishing
3411 Preston Rd. Ste. C-13-a46
Frisco, Texas

ISBN#978-1-945693-16-8

*The names of people and their stories have been changed where I felt it was necessary to do so.

ACKNOWLEDGMENTS

Jesus—I could never put into words what You have done for me. My life is Yours.

To my family—Erica, Elisha, Jasmine, Carissa, and Micah—honored to have a front row seat to your lives—it's my honor to tell your "stories."

TABLE OF CONTENTS

PREFACE

"The kingdom of God is not a matter of talk, but of power"
(1 Corinthians 4:20).

"When they saw the BOLDNESS of Peter and John, and
perceived they were UNEDUCATED and UNTRAINED men,
they marveled and realized they had BEEN WITH JESUS"
(Acts 4:13, 14).

"Jesus answered and said to them, 'You are mistaken, not
knowing the Scriptures nor the power of God'"
(Matthew 22:29).

"Ruined For Normal" describes a lifestyle that makes
the 'impossible' attractive! It lets the Holy Spirit lead us and
guide us in all things—not just the 'every day' existing most
Christians have accepted.

This book's purpose is to stir up a fresh hunger for
salvations, signs, wonders, healings, and miracles. It will
present the balance you need between operating in the super-
natural and living a lifestyle of godly character with a solid
biblical foundation. It will challenge the reader to look for
dangerous places because dangerous places are safe places in
the Kingdom.

INTRODUCTION

Grandparents delivering addicts in a crack house.

Teenagers releasing prophetic words to married couples.

College students demonstrating healing to the blind.

Men and Women leaving wicked lifestyles and becoming separated to Him.

Toddlers carrying authority over what was once said to be incurable.

RUINED shares the stories of the willing, not the spiritually elite. It is a collection of responses to promptings of the Holy Spirit and a map to develop a lifestyle of godly character and Divine encounters. Jesus is using not only the 'least likely,' but He is also using them in unusual ways—in unordinary places—to touch people who least expect it. These brave ones have been "Ruined."

The world looks at what has been ruined and immediately decreases its value and ability, but in the Kingdom it carries a different meaning. When someone truly encountered Jesus, they were never the same. They ended up looking and living just like He did. They were ruined!

With this lens, being Ruined brings increase, value, and authority. You become ruined for normal because easy and comfortable does not satisfy the appetite any longer.

When you see sickness, you know you are called to heal it!
When you see brokenness, you have a compassion to restore!
When you see injustice, you are stirred to correct it!

The wheel chairs, negativity, crutches, bitterness, and bruises that used to be avoided are now difficult to ignore because the love and power of Jesus is drawing you to minister to those who struggle with them.

Just like the Jesus Who "ruined" you, He is wanting to use you to do the same thing. The Ruined are rising with young Samuels, who hear the voice of the Lord at an early age and whose words never fall to the ground. They are contending for the days where classrooms turn to prayer rooms, boardrooms seek heavenly wisdom, and corruption becomes extinct. They're dreaming of the headlines that are written of cancer centers and rehab centers being shut down in cities because of a lack of patients. History will and is being written by the Ruined.

You've heard the call. Now it's time to respond. Let's pray together before you go any further:

Jesus,
I am grateful that Your desire is to know me and bring increase to my life. I surrender everything I am to You, and ask You to ruin me. I declare I will have a greater spiritual hunger for You, Your Word, and Your assignment on my life. As I journey with You through this message,

I decree I will have an increased awareness of Your presence and a clarity to hear Your voice. At the end of all of it, I want to be so ruined that I look just like You.

Ruin me, Lord!

In Your Name I ask these things. Amen.

Chapter 1

I'VE BEEN RUINED

"Where's my car?" my friend asked, as I was walking her back to her car after we had finished a prayer meeting at a local high school. When we arrived near the spot where she had previously parked, she looked around and asked again, "Where's my car?"

I looked around as well, "Did you park right here?" I motioned to the empty spot in front of us.

"Yes!"

"Are you sure you parked *right here*?"

"Yes! I parked right here!"

"Well, you can't park here. It's a no-parking zone." I said, pointing to the bright red sign above us.

"They don't mean that!"

"Apparently they do because your car is no longer here ... better call the number on the sign to find out where your car ended up," I responded, a bit sarcastically at this point.

A quick phone call later and we find out that sure enough, her car had been towed and impounded. Knowing I had nothing else going on that morning, I offered to give her a ride to the car lot.

We pulled into a huge, dirt lot of impounded cars and parked in front of a double-wide trailer. As soon as we entered the trailer, the door behind us slammed shut, taking all the sunshine along with it. My friend and I stood shoulder-to-shoulder, staring down the dark corridor ahead of us. There was a single light bulb flickering ahead ... in the distance ... alright, the situation was getting a little creepy!

Suddenly a large, hulking figure appeared under the flickering light bulb and yelled, "AYE, What do ya'll want?"

Nope.

I turned to my friend, "That," I said, as I pointed to the figure, "is talking to you."

She explained how she was the one calling about the Silver Volvo.

"You're the one who parked in a NO Parking Zone? How come you parked in a No-Parking Zone? It said NO Parking. Stop parking in No Parking Zone!" the mysterious creature bellowed down the hallway. (Just to remind you, at this point, we still had no idea who or what we were talking to.)

He proceeded to look over his shoulder and continued, "JIMMY! Aye, Jimmy-run-around-back-and-pull-that-car-up-right-quick-yeah-the-one-from-this-morning-the-silver-one-no-not-that-one-the-silver-Volvo-Jimmy."

He then turned back to face us, "We'll-get-your-car-pulled-around-right-quick-just-stop-parking-in-NO-parking-zones!" He said all of this in what seemed like the span of one breath.

I think we were still a little shocked by the slaughterhouse vibes this trailer was giving us. That, along with being yelled at by what we think is a man, led us to stay motionless and silent as all of this was unfolding. Seeing as he wasn't going to get a

14

response, the hulking figure returned to a back office, while we waited for Jimmy to return with the car.

Now, I'm sure we all have those Christian friends who are crazy. You know, the ones who try to find demons in trees, or popsicles? Well the tribe I grew up around was a little like this—always ready for anything. So it shouldn't have been a surprise to me when my friend (very suddenly) broke the silence of the slaughterhouse trailer and said, "Chris!"

"What's up?" I responded, a little off-guard.

I noticed then that she had that spiritual twitch in her eye as she declared, "Chris, we have been sent here by the Lord!"

Knowing she was about to do something crazy, something that probably meant my spiritual comfort zone was about to be invaded, I quickly said, "No, no, no! YOU'VE been sent here by the Lord; I knew where to park!"

She poked me on the shoulder and shot back, "Stop playing! I'm serious!"

To which, I countered, "You. Stop. Playing!"

"C'mon, I *feel* something. Let's pray and see what happens!"

I did what any other Christian in my situation would have done. I pretended to pray. (Oh come on, we've all done it!) So, I bowed my head, closed my eyes, and nodded every now and then. If I'm being honest, I was trying to buy time—hoping that Jimmy would show up with the car before things got out of hand. In the midst of my performance, the Lord's voice broke through, and I heard Him say, "Son, I want you to wash that man's feet."

I cringed and thought, "Oh, Lord, not You, too!"

Again, "Son, I want you to wash that man's feet."

I motioned my hand towards myself, as if asking the Lord to come closer so we could share a secret.

"First off, we don't even know what 'that' is. Second, you want me to wash *its* feet?! I'll do anything for You, Lord, but I ain't washing its feet."

Again, "Son, I want you to wash that man's feet."

I fired back sarcastically, "You know what, You created *it*, You wash his feet!"

Without delay, I felt the Divine pressure of His original words, "Son, I want you to wash that man's feet."

I finally surrender and threw my hands in the air. "Fine!"

I didn't realize that this whole time it looked like I was murmuring to myself, while making weird hand motions. My friend looked at me in silent confusion as I made my way to the kitchen area of the trailer. There, I found a crusty looking coffee mug and a bowl. I filled it with cold water and went back to where my friend waited. Now, I had done a few foot washings by that point to know that you wanted warm water, not cold water. But cold water was all they had, and I remember thinking that as soon as I poured this cold water on that man's hoof, he was probably going to punch me in the throat!

Finally, the man walked back to where we were standing and made his way to an office chair in the corner of the room. As he sat, he took one more jab at us, shaking his head as he said, "Can't believe you parked in a No Parking Zone."

My friend looked at me, and I looked at her. She gave

16

me a little shove forward, and I sheepishly addressed the man saying, "Sir, I'm sorry about that.

"But listen ...

"We're Christians.

"And God speaks to us.

"And He told me,

"That He wants me.

"To wash.

"Ya feet."

I felt as if my mouth was full of sand after I said those words.

The man looked incredibly confused as he sat up and pointed a finger at himself. With a half laugh he asked, "You want to wash ... my feet?"

While shaking my head no, I replied, "Yes, sir."

His quiet response shocked me. "Ok," was all he said.

I knelt down in front of him and started to unlace his shoes. I'm pretty sure I know what death smells like—this man's shoes! As I went to take his socks off I noticed they didn't slide off, but rather, peeled off ... like a banana! As my fingers brushed the back of his heels, they were as dry as the El Paso desert. When I saw the top of his feet, I realized this man had the hairiest feet I had ever seen in my life. His foot-hair was so long in fact, that if a breeze came through, it would have been blowing in the wind. As if all of that wasn't discouraging enough, when I got to his toes—he had one toe that was yellow ... yellow! Not just yellow, but glow-in-the-dark, highlighter, radioactive yellow!

Before I lost my nerve, I put the bowl under his feet, grabbed the mug with cold water and started to pour it over his feet. I remember feeling all the dirt and grime wash off. I watched as clear water turned to black-gray. The Lord then led me to pray for him, and I never forgot how I started my prayer.

"Lord! These feet have seen some rough years!" But I felt something trigger in my heart and continued, "But I feel like these are years the devil has stolen from him. In fact, he is separated from his wife and he is worried about losing his two sons. I declare this marriage to be healed, and I break the generational curse of divorce off of his family. I declare that he will be a committed husband and a devoted father who will show his sons a godly example of manhood and show his sons what a God-honoring marriage looks like."

As I continued to pray, this man burst into tears and began to weep uncontrollably. Jesus was interrupting this man's pain and weakness with overwhelming love.

Moments later, I heard my friend's car being pulled up, and this man quickly asked if we could stop. He thanked us, but said he didn't want his co-worker to see him in that condition. Remembering he and I weren't the only ones in the room, I locked eyes with my friend. I could tell she was just as shocked as I was! The man thanked us again, my friend paid her fine, and we parted ways.

My heart was still beating fast, and my mind was still reeling by the time I got in my car. I sat there and said, "Lord, that was cool, but You can't do that to me! That was way too unexpected! I mean how am I suppose to live now after experiencing that!? I can never be the same. How am I supposed to be normal?" I remember yelling, "Lord, you're ruining me!"

He immediately broke through my tantrum and shouted, "Exactly! I never called you to be normal. Son, I am ruining you for normal!" And He has been true to His word ever since.

DO YOU REALIZE?

Do you realize that God has been ruining you for "normal" since the day you met Him? As a Pastor, what used to frustrate me the most was having to watch too many people encounter God at a powerful service or conference and then a few weeks later see them go right back to "normal." It was confusing to watch them worship with such passion, respond to the Word with such hunger, and walk away with a Divine focus, only to see them lose it all in a couple of weeks. It wasn't until I read 2 John 1:8 that clarity was given to me; it reads:

"Watch out that you do not lose what we have worked for, but that you may be rewarded fully"
(2 John 1:8, NASB).

John is reminding us that your encounter should make you an encounter for Jesus! Many people don't feel like they did when they encountered Him. Not because it wasn't a real or true encounter, but because they did nothing with that encounter and went back to "normal." Once you meet Jesus, you can't help but be ruined. He never leaves anyone the same way He found them. He is habitual in ruining us for good, so we start to develop a new normal.

19

We can draw some insight from the life of the Apostle Peter on being "ruined." Acts, chapter 3, shows us a defining moment in Peter's life. All of us have had these kinds of moments; some of them mark us for good, and then, there are some of them that we'd rather forget. If I can be honest, I am extremely grateful for Peter because I see so much of myself in his story. I feel like if God can love Peter, He can love anyone! Let's look at some of Peter's defining moments.

Peter is the first of the disciples to recognize and declare that Jesus is the "Christ, the Son of the living God" (Matthew 16:16), but later he is caught arguing about who's the greatest in the kingdom (Luke 9:46). Peter famously walks on the water with Jesus, only to start sinking moments later (Matthew 14:29) Peter even boldly declares, "Lord I'll die for you!" (Matthew 26:35), only to deny knowing Jesus hours later (Luke 22:54-62). We all can identify with Peter; he has his good moments and his not-so-good moments. I am happy to report that Acts, chapter 3, is a good moment for Peter, it reads:

> *"Now Peter and John went up together to the temple at the hour of prayer, the ninth hour. And a certain man lame from his mother's womb was carried, who the people laid daily at the gate of the temple which is called Beautiful, to ask alms from those who entered the temple; who, seeing Peter and John about to go into the temple, asked for alms. And fixing his eyes on him, with John, Peter said, 'Look at us.' So he gave them his attention, expecting to receive something*

20

from them. Then Peter said, 'Silver and gold I do not have, but what I do have I give you: In the name of Jesus Christ of Nazareth, rise up and walk.' And he took him by the right hand and lifted him up, and immediately his feet and ankle bones received strength. So he, leaping up, stood and walked and entered the temple with them— walking, leaping, and praising God. And all the people saw him walking and praising God. Then they knew that it was he who sat begging alms at the Beautiful Gate of the temple; and they were filled with wonder and amazement at what had happened to him" (Acts 3:1-10).

The Peter we're reading about here is different than the one I described earlier. This Peter is spiritually sensitive, is available, even in the middle of what would be a routine prayer schedule, and is a risk taker. How did Peter get this way? I believe it's because he had been ruined, and he learned to stay ruined. The Apostle Peter would become vital in establishing the Church of Jesus Christ. He would bring clarity to the fact that Gentiles can receive salvation, alongside the children of Israel, and would demonstrate and defend the baptism of the Holy Spirit.

His epistles show the perfect picture of a lifestyle of holiness, grace, and truth. He prophetically said that false teachers would rise, and he warned against them. He was given insight and revelation on how to handle unfair treatment and persecution; and he did it in a way that would not only result in bringing honor to Jesus, but also in being blessed. He raised the dead, walked in such authority that even his "shadow" would heal people and those who lied to the Holy Spirit would fall dead at his feet.

Eventually he would be crucified, but he held the death of Jesus in such high regard, that he chose to be crucified upside down. Does any of this sound like the man who argued with Jesus about who was the greatest? The man who started to sink while walking on water, and denied Jesus three times? No! This new Peter had been ruined.

I believe the three and half years Peter spent with Jesus were critical in his development, but nothing that he encountered could compare to the impact of one key moment in his life. Let me set this up for you. In John, chapter 13, Peter is shocked to hear Jesus declare that He was going to be betrayed, arrested, and handed over to His enemies to be killed. Peter passionately says he would do the same and would follow Jesus to the end. Jesus sobers Peter's passion by revealing Peter's soon denial, "By the time the rooster crows you will deny me three times" (John 13:38).

In John, chapter 18, these prophetic words were fulfilled—First, Peter denies he knows Jesus to a servant girl, next at the door to the temple to another servant girl, and finally while he's warming himself by the fire, a crowd of people recognized him as one of Jesus' followers. Peter bitterly denies the claims and even started calling curses down on Jesus (Matthew 26:74, Mark 14:71).

Just after Peter's third and final denial, he hears the rooster crow. No doubt Jesus' words replayed in his mind at this exact moment. We know the rest of the story. Jesus goes on to be wrongfully accused, judged, beaten, humiliated and crucified for all of our sins. Peter's crushed, realizing that Jesus is dead and there was nothing he could do to bring Him back. There is such a huge difference between the Peter we see here and the Peter we see in Acts 3, but the Divine turnaround that would ruin Peter for the rest of his life didn't come until John, chapter 21.

> *"After this, Jesus appeared again to the disciples, this time at the Tiberias Sea (the Sea of Galilee). This is how he did it: Simon Peter, Thomas (nicknamed "Twin"), Nathanael from Cana in Galilee, the brothers Zebedee, and two other disciples were together. Simon Peter announced,* **'I'm going fishing.'**
>
> *"The rest of them replied,* **'We're going with you.'** *They went out and got in the boat. They caught nothing that night. When the sun came up, Jesus was standing on the beach, but they didn't recognize him.*
>
> *"Jesus spoke to them: 'Good morning! Did you catch anything for breakfast?'*
>
> *"They answered, 'No.'*
>
> *"He said, 'Throw the net off the right side of the boat and see what happens.'*

"They did what he said. All of a sudden there were so many fish in it, they weren't strong enough to pull it in.

"Then the disciple Jesus loved said to Peter, 'It's the Master!'

"When Simon Peter realized that it was the Master, he threw on some clothes, for he was stripped for work, and dove into the sea. *The other disciples came in by boat for they weren't far from land, a hundred yards or so, pulling along the net full of fish. When they got out of the boat, they saw a fire laid, with fish and bread cooking on it"* (John 21:1-9, The Message, emphasis mine).

Let's focus on Peter's announcement in verse 3, "I'm going fishing." He's not announcing that he's hungry or that he's bored so he's going fishing. He is letting the disciples know, "I am going back to what I used to be because I've lost it all and have nothing else to do with my life, so I might as well go back to the life I used to know—I'm going fishing." Peter is going back to normal.

My heart breaks to write this because the same is true for so many today, when they encounter failure, frustration, or the unexpected. Like Peter, we go back to old habits, relationships, and lifestyles, which only serve to suffocate all that God has done in our lives. You must realize that God is ruining you for normal! To go back would only unravel everything the Lord has

24

done for you and cause spiritual amnesia to the point where you can no longer recall the destiny He has for your life.

It even says in verse 4, "Jesus was standing on the beach, but the disciples didn't recognize Him." How is this even possible? They had spent the last three and half years being up close and involved in everything Jesus was doing. They watched Jesus heal the sick, feed the hungry, raise the dead, and shut down every argument the religious elite ever threw at him. Yet, the disciples, including Peter, didn't recognize him? Going back to normal is the only thing that causes this level of forgetfulness.

Jesus began appearing to His disciples, including Peter, just days before (John 20:19-29). Peter sees Jesus after He was resurrected at least twice and still makes the choice to go back to normal. Why? Because he felt the failure of not following through with what he promised, combined with denying Jesus three times, filled his heart with more regret than remembering every promise and word Jesus gave to him.

One definition for regret is when your past is too much for you to carry, and it steals the life out of those who desire "the ruined life." Peter let his regret and shame lead him back to what he used to be, a fisherman, rather than carrying on his true identity, purpose, and assignment, which was to be a Fisher of Men. Going back to old ways is easy to do, but there is a great danger, it's contagious. Look at verse 3 again. Peter declares, "I am going fishing!" and the rest of the disciples quickly respond, "We're going with you!"

The decisions and directions of our lives affect those in

our sphere of influence. It's not just us who can be lured into going back to normal, but everyone we influence, as well. For the sake of your future and the destinies of those around you, don't go back to normal! Live your life with no regrets, never to return to your old thought patterns and fruitless lifestyles that keep you busy, yet produce nothing of eternal value. I can't remind you enough, He is ruining you for normal!"

HE KNOWS WHERE TO FIND YOU

The disciples may not have recognized him, but Jesus knew where to find them. John 21:4 says, "Jesus was standing on the shore." Jesus is not afraid to show up on your shore. Your painful shores of regret, shame, and failure. I don't care how dirty your sin is or how great your betrayal to Him was, He is not intimidated to show up on your shores!

I will always remember when I felt similar to Peter. In June of 1999, I got saved, filled with the Holy Spirit, and was called into ministry all in one night. I was eager to fulfill my call and couldn't wait to attend Christ For The Nations Institute in Dallas, Texas, after I graduated high school. At the time, I was in a serious relationship, so serious that we were engaged to be married. I was also asked to help lead our Junior High School ministry, which I was thrilled about. I thought I had it all; I found someone to spend the rest of my life with and was starting to walk in my calling, what more could I want?

So I put off going to CFNI for one year to see where God would lead this new opportunity. Yet, behind the scenes, things weren't that innocent. I had a massive anger problem, which isn't a healthy trait when you're serving people. The pressure of leading and building would cause my anger to be directed toward the girl I was engaged to, which almost always resulted in a fight.

If it wasn't my anger that was triggered, it was my addiction to pornography. Which then led me to pressure her into sleeping with me. I'm embarrassed to admit this, but I would consider my weakest moments to be after our Junior High services. If I didn't preach well or if something didn't go right, it would throw me into a rage that would lead to another yelling match or my insecurity would scream and I ran to the only thing I wanted to be comforted by—my flesh.

My Pastors quickly noticed this pattern and did the right thing by asking me to step down. I was devastated and blamed everyone in the world for what happened, but I never took responsibility for my issues. I isolated myself in the following months and started to spiral down. I hit rock bottom when one evening, my fiancé and I got into a huge fight. I drove off crying and called my mother, wondering how my life had gotten so out of control while I was trying to serve the vision God had put in my heart.

Like only a mother could, she reminded me, "Son, God hasn't changed His mind about you. You've been so distracted from what He originally told you to do, you need to be at CFNI."

That was all I needed. I put in my two-weeks-notice, packed everything I had into two trash bags, and made plans to leave. Yet again though, I would find a way to get myself into a mess. I can totally relate to Peter, two steps forward … five

27

steps backwards!

The night before I was to leave for CFNI, I called my ex-fiancé, and asked her to come over so we could smooth things over. Big mistake! I ended up convincing her and myself that what we needed was time away from each other, but that we should still keep our relationship going. The next morning I drove to Dallas feeling like things were finally starting to turn-around, but a long-distance relationship, mixed with an anger issue, while adding a big splash of perversion, is not the recipe for a great romance. It didn't take long until I was back in my old patterns, cycles, and habits.

I can remember cussing out her out on the phone, hanging up on her, and then returning to class to hear more about how I was going to change the world and be a phenomenal pastor. I became the biggest introvert, which is not like me. I remember being so possessive and controlling that often my calls to her weren't to wish her a great day; it was to find out who she was with and where she was going. Our fighting got worse, but I was so addicted to the relationship that I was willing to ignore all the warning signs and the concern and caution from those around me.

I fell into a deep depression that was so bad all I wanted to do was sleep so I didn't have to feel the void and pain I carried with me. Needless to say, the relationship didn't last long. I returned home for spring break only to erupt into an argument, which ended in a goodbye for good. I was crushed, but instead of taking responsibility for my actions, I began to disqualify and belittle everything God had told me to do with my life. I lost direction for my life and had no desire to fulfill my destiny. I daily felt like a hypocrite and a failure because everything I heard in my classes would only convince me I had messed up too much. I believed I was damaged goods. How could God ever use me or even want me?

If I had it my way, I would have jumped back in my car and drove back home to "fix" the relationship, but as it turns out, as soon as I got back to my dorm my car broke down. (Sometimes He allows life to corner us so we can finally see how much we need Him). I couldn't physically run away, but I was still running away in my heart. I didn't realize it, but God had cornered me with love and let me "go fishing" all night, only to meet me on the shore of my mess.

The next day I went to a night service we had at school. I walked in heavy, broken, and with no way to fix my problems. I had nothing to offer Jesus that night, but the worst version of myself. Worship began, and I found myself in front of the auditorium, sobbing. I still remember feeling those tears roll down my face and soak the carpet. I was completely undone.

As I closed my eyes, I had a vision; I saw myself worshipping at the front in the condition I was in, but then I saw Jesus walking down the center aisle. He was carrying a bowl of water and a towel. Anticipating disappointment to be all over His face, He surprised me. He looked at me with kindest eyes and warmest countenance. It was then I noticed my body; I was covered in bruises and stains and had bleeding wounds all over me.

The sight of my brokenness never changed His demeanor. He took His towel, dipped it in the water, and began to wash me. As soon as He wiped an area, what was dirty was made clean and what was bleeding was healed. He was thorough and didn't miss a single spot. His willingness to be around me at my worst undid my pain and shame better than my regret and isolation ever could. He was "ruining" me.

While He attended to each area, my attention was further drawn to not only how clean He was making me, but also how bright He was making me shine. My tears began to dry up and I couldn't help but smile back at Him. Once He was done, He looked me straight in the eyes. He didn't say anything, but His look said everything. He then pointed at my heart, smiled even bigger, and walked away.

I came out of this vision in the middle of worship, but everything had changed. My voice had a volume to sing I hadn't had in a long time. My praise had a dance and a joy to it I didn't realize I had been missing. Jesus had come to my shore. I was ruined.

John 21:4 says, "When the sun came up, Jesus was standing on the shore, but they didn't recognize him." Let me remind you that regret, shame, and failure cause spiritual amnesia. Once you start to live out of these, you will begin to walk toward the same things Peter, the disciples, and myself went back to. But aren't you glad we serve a God Who isn't afraid to show up on our shores!?

I don't care how messed you are and have been, Jesus is not afraid to get in the middle of your junk! I don't care what the latest statistics say about you or even what people in your life have spoken over, God is ruining you!

The devil will do everything he can to get you to "go back to fishing," so you can live your life distracted and filled with bitterness and resentment. I believe at this moment the devil thought, "Not only did I get Jesus, but now I get to sabotage Peter, too."

But then Jesus showed up on Peter's shore! John 21:7 says that once Peter realized it was Jesus on the shore, he forgot about the catch all fishermen dream of catching and dove into the sea. Some say the swim was about 100 yards. The devil must have been working over-time during that swim. Bombarding Peter's mind with thoughts and reminders of his sin, shame, and failure. Tirelessly trying to slow Peter's swim to a halt, enticing him with old patterns, habits, and cycles. Peter just kept his legs pumping hard and his arms slicing through the water.

I can't imagine what went through Satan's thoughts when he saw Jesus standing on the beach with Peter racing towards Him. It probably went something like, "This can't happen! No! If Peter looks into Jesus' eyes again, it's over, I'll lose him!"

Out of breath, Peter makes it to the shore, only to realize Jesus wasn't there to reject him, but to ruin him to the point of no return! I think I have a pretty good idea of how Jesus looked at Peter and the exchange that happened between them. What Peter encountered is what I encountered. That is what Jesus is offering you right now—a ruined life!

A RADICAL RESPONSE

The Bible and church history have made known the rest of Peter's life, but what isn't known is what will be recorded of your life. If you are reading this right now and you feel the hand of God pulling you toward Him, He is not bringing you close to reject you or embarrass you. He wants to embrace you and ruin you for normal.

Peter went "fishing" because he was going back to his old lifestyle, but produced nothing. John 21:3 deliberately records they fished all night and "caught nothing." Then, the next morning Jesus intentionally asks, "Did you catch anything?" It's almost as if when Jesus asks this, what he was really asking Peter was, "Son, how's it going, trying to do life without me? Have you noticed you'll produce nothing?"

Notice Peter fished all night and caught nothing, but when Jesus said, "Cast your nets," he brings in a catch so big that the disciples weren't strong enough to pull it in. What a picture we have of Peter doing life in his own strength; yet, accomplishing nothing without Jesus. But when he listened to Jesus' command, he secured a record-breaking catch. This is part of being ruined.

I'm sure Peter could have looked at this miracle catch and thought, "I still got it." He could have taken that massive catch and started up his fishing business again. It would have been easy to read too much into this once-in-a-life-time catch and be convinced that the will of God for his life was to fish. But John 21:7 reminds us that when Peter realized it was Jesus, he jumped into the sea and swam to be with Jesus on the shore. He rejected a normal life, gave a radical response, and was ruined forever. He wasn't willing to deny Jesus a fourth time.

I'm not asking you to be casual in your response; I'm challenging you to be extreme and undignified. Stop caring about what people may think or what people may say. Let us all draw from Peter's life and give the appropriate radical response. If you need help with what that looks like, please go to Appendix A in the back of this book. There is a starting place to a ruined life, and you'll find the explanation there.

DANGEROUS PLACES

In the next chapter, you will discover that the "ruined life" doesn't always lead you to safe places, but to dangerous ones. Because you have been ruined, you will notice an appetite for the impossible begin to develop inside of you. Welcome to your new normal!

Chapter 2

A NEW NORMAL

I will always remember the day God told me, "Son, I need you to go and visit that psychic." I knew instantly where and who He was referring to. Just down the road from my office was a "Psychic/Palm Reader" shop. I would pass this place almost every day on my way to work, and most days, I would stretch out my hand and say a quick prayer as I drove by. My prayer would be simple: "Lord, I lift the veil off of those people and declare that they would look to you for life and hope." This became routine—pray, pass the shop, and keep driving until it was out sight and out of mind. Except, when one day, things changed.

It was this particular day, when I drove by the Psychic Shop, I heard the Lord say to me, "I gave you hands, but I also gave you a mouth." I thought, "That's weird," and I kept on driving.

As soon as I got settled into my office, I immediately felt the presence of God. He said, "Son, I need you to go and visit that Psychic."

Confused at His command, I said, "Lord, did You hear Yourself? You want me to do *what*?"

He repeated it a second time, "Son, I need you to go and visit that Psychic."

To which I quickly replied, "Lord, I don't have time

for that. I've got phone calls I need to return, emails I need to respond to, and if I go, I'll back up the appointments I had scheduled for today."

He became silent, but I could feel His strong gaze putting holy pressure on my heart. I have learned that when He is this persistent, the best thing for me to do is to follow through with what He just said. So I grabbed my things, walked out of my office and said to my assistant, "I'll be right back; I've got to go and visit this Psychic." Any other assistant would have been confused, but not mine, she knows I'm crazy! They're used to my wife and me living like this.

She just naturally replied, "Ok, cool."

Now, I'm a planner. I like lists, structure, and post it notes. Since this expedition was not in my plans, I was starting to get irritated. As I drove towards the shop I said, "Lord, this is a waste of my time. I have so much hitting me all at once right now. I need to be focused, and this is just a waste of my time. What am I suppose to even tell this person? At least let me know that."

But He remained silent. I pulled up to the shop, but was too embarrassed to park in the front. I was concerned one of my students or co-workers would see me coming and going from this place and think, "Oh, so now I know where Pastor Chris gets all his messages from." (Our imagination can be too active sometimes). Again I asked the Lord what He wanted me to say or if there was a message I was supposed to deliver, but received the same response, silence. But I was committed to be faithful, even if that meant looking foolish.

Fighting the reminders going off in my head about how this was a waste of my time, I knocked on the door. A man immediately opened the door and said, "What do you want?"

I'm 100 percent sure I froze for a minute, not expecting him to answer so fast. He repeated himself, "What do you want?"

In the most awkward voice possible, I stuttered out, "Hhhhiiiiieeee."

He just stared at me and asked again, "What do you want?" This time I managed to get a little more out,

"Hieeee, I'm Chris, I work down the road and I wanted to ask you some questions."

"Questions about what?" He shot back defensively.

"About your business."

"For what?" He now sounded annoyed.

By now I'm thinking, "Okay, Lord, now would be a good time to tell me why I'm here and what I should be saying!"

Since I didn't answer him right away, he tried again, "Excuse me, why do you want to know about my business?"

I still had no idea why I was there, so I said, "I'm just interested, I'll pay you for your time!"

His countenance and approach completely changed, "Oh! Please come on in. Would you like something to drink?" (It's true what they say, money talks!)

I walked past several rooms expecting to see people levitating, brooms sweeping on their own, and Ouija boards to be giving messages, but it looked like a normal home with nice furniture. We sat on a couch and he said, "So what questions would you like to ask me?"

Still, not really sure where this was going, I asked the first thing that came to mind. "How long have you been a Psychic Palm Reader?"

He then began to tell me how for the last 20 years he had this shop, but his family went back three generations of Psychic Palm Readers. Bragging he added, "Yeah, my family can see 60 to 90 days in the future. Here, give me your hand I'll prove it." He started reaching for my hands when I quickly pulled back.

"Sir, that's ok, I'm pretty confident about my future. In fact, we have something in common. The Lord has used me to share with people when they are to expect babies, or when they're going to make career changes, or even major life decisions."

He squinted his eyes at me and said, "Oh I see. You're a Christian aren't you?"

"Yes sir I am."

He surprised me when he leaned back against his seat, and said with a big smile, "So am I!" He continued, "Jesus Christ is my Lord and Savior, and it's the power of the Holy Spirit that gives me the ability to do what I do."

With a grin on my face and my eyebrows raised, I replied, "Really? Well I don't think we serve the same Jesus, but we can get to that later."

My spirit began connecting the dots, and I said, "Sir, I drive by this place and always pray for you. Today, I did what I always do and stretched out my hand toward your business and prayed for you, but God reminded He didn't just give me hands, he gave me a mouth, too." With boldness rising inside of me, I continued, "Sir, I was in my office and God told me to come and visit you. I wasn't sure why, but now I know. Sir, would you allow me to pray for you?"

As I went to gently put my hands on him, he slapped my hand away screaming, "Don't you touch me! Don't touch me! I'll lose it if you touch me! This is over, it's time for you to leave."

He stood up quickly and started to march me out the door. I hadn't been in there for more than three minutes, and I was already getting kicked out! Like a ninja, I broke free and tried again, "Sir, please! Let me pray for you!"

He opened his front door and started pushing me out. As he went to slam the door, I put my foot in between the door and the doorframe, causing him to shut the door on my foot instead. I put my face in the 3-inch gap, created by my foot and the door, and shouted, "SIR! Please let me pray for you!"

He responded by kicking my shin, which caused me to move my foot, and he slammed the door in my face.

I was embarrassed, upset, and confused. I looked up to Heaven and sarcastically said, "Go and visit the Psychic," You said. "I gave you hands, but I also gave you a mouth," You said. Lord! I told You that was a waste of my time!"

Finally, the Spirit of God spoke to me, "Son I didn't want to show him something, I wanted to show *you* something." His response tempered my edge, He continued, "Son, I wanted to show you what a counterfeit does when it's contending with the real deal! I'm not looking for people who can just take risks in church services. I am looking for those who are willing to go from psychic shop to crack house to boardroom. I'm looking for those who are surrendered enough so that I can break through the routine of their day. That at a moment's notice I can give them an assignment they will be faithful to carry out. I want to be able to call on you like this."

This sent a shockwave through my heart. I found myself in Peter's story again. From chapter 1, we now understand what it means to "be ruined," but what does it look like to have a Ruined Life? How do we pursue a radical life when everything around us is so ordinary?

Let's look at Acts, chapter 3, again with a ruined perspective:

> *"Now Peter and John went up together to the temple at **the hour of prayer, the ninth hour**. And a certain man **lame from his mother's womb** was carried, who **the people laid daily** at the gate of the temple which is called Beautiful, to ask alms from those who entered the temple; who, seeing Peter and John about to go into the temple, asked for alms. And **fixing his eyes on him**, with John, Peter said, 'Look at us.' So he gave them his attention, expecting to receive something from them. Then Peter said, '**Silver and gold I do not have, but what I do have I give you: In the name of Jesus Christ of Nazareth, rise up and walk.**' And he took him by the right hand and lifted him up, and immediately his feet and ankle*

bones received strength. So he, leaping up, stood and walked and entered the temple with them— walking, leaping, and praising God. And all the people saw him walking and praising God. Then they knew that it was he who sat begging alms at the Beautiful Gate of the temple; and they were filled with wonder and amazement at what had happened to him" (Acts 3:1-10).

By now, Peter has been living a ruined lifestyle, but here we see the fruit of a "ruined life." Just like my situation with the Psychic, Peter is going about his daily routine, entering the temple to pray like he has always done. Except this time is different, because he has been ruined for normal and now has a "ruined life" perspective. To understand the text above we need to ask, how routine was this for Peter and this beggar? In Verse 2 it says, "The hour of prayer, the ninth hour," which we know to be 3 p.m. For Peter this was expected behavior because it was customary for the Jewish people to pray three times a day. Since childhood Peter had entered the temple, so we can also ascertain this isn't the first time he has ever seen this beggar as he entered. In fact, in Acts 3:2 it also says they, "laid this man daily at the gate of the temple to beg."

How long had this man been laid daily at the gate? Acts 4:22 records he was laid there for 40 years. This beggar was a familiar face to Peter. So what made this time different than all the other times Peters saw him? Peter had been ruined and was now living the ruined life. Let's refresh ourselves with the

highlights of Peter's Journey:
- John 18—Peter denies Jesus three times
- John 21—Jesus showed up on his shores to restore him
- Acts 1—He learned to wait for the Promise, which is the Baptism of the Holy Spirit.
- Acts 2—Holy Spirit is poured out on Peter, who preaches Jesus to the same crowd that just crucified Him and 3,000 were saved.

What made this time different was Peter was living the ruined life now! I love how it says in verse 4 that Peter, "fixed his eyes on him." In other words, he looked at this man with a different set of options. Peter had a choice. He could keep going with his spiritual routine or he could reject normal. With this beggar being a familiar face, Peter could have thought, "Well, he's always been that way," but the ruined lifestyle he was living said, "This man can be healed!"

We must challenge ourselves to start looking at our city with a different set of options. May we reject normal and start looking at the sick and addicted with a different set of options. When we walk in the ruined life, we begin to look at people and situations with a different set of options.

JUST BE NORMAL

I believe the constant lie that's being whispered to those pursuing the ruined life isn't, "Don't pray for the sick" or "Don't believe for the impossible." I believe we're baited today with the lie of "Just be normal. This is the way it's always been and things will never change. Stop dreaming; you can't see transformation in your day. Things will always be this way."

Friend, if God wanted you to be normal, then He should never have sent Jesus. He should never have sent the Holy Spirit, and He should never have equipped you with your Bible! I believe you're reading this book because you're tired of what's being called normal in your school, city, and region. You're tired of 'business as usual' and the way things are is not okay with you. It's because the ruined life puts a holy discomfort on the inside of you as you look at people and situations with heaven's perspective. The ruined ones approach everything with a different set of options!

NOT EVERYTHING IS AUTOMATIC

I think a second lie that ruined ones will face is "everything in God's Kingdom is automatic, and I don't have to pay any cost for it." This is so far from the truth. Let me share how God spoke this into my life.

I was getting ready to minister at a conference when I went to the restroom to wash my hands. I walked in completely focused on the message God had given me for this gathering, and as I went to the sink, I realized the soap dispenser was automatic. I thought, "Hey, that's cool," and then the water faucet was automatic, as well, so I figured there was a pattern here. But when I went to put my hands under the dryer, nothing happened.

I didn't realize that I had been standing there for quite some time with my hands dripping wet; yet, thinking over what

I was about to preach. I looked to see if the dryer had been unplugged, but it wasn't. I even tried putting my hand up the spout to see if it was clogged. Of course, it wasn't. With my arms shoved in the dryer, I noticed there was a big silver button that said, "Push here." I quickly thanked God no one else was in the restroom to see what had just happened. Right then God dropped this truth in my heart, "Son, not everything in My Kingdom is automatic."

Salvation, that's free. Holy Spirit, He's free. Grace, that's free. But obedience, that will cost you. Spiritual discipline, that will cost you. Faithfulness, that will cost you. But when you are living the ruined life, you are never focused on the cost, but the reward because you look at everything with a different set of options.

DANGEROUS PLACES

You can see this in Acts 3:4 when Peter says to the beggar, "Look at us." Peter was settling into his new lifestyle. Losing awareness of his surroundings, passing by the hurt and broken was no longer permitted by his ruined lifestyle. This is where the ruined recognize that dangerous places are safe places in the Kingdom! When you walk in the ruined life, you now have a warrior way of thinking. You don't find use for words like "can't, won't, shouldn't, or impossible" because you are built by God to stay in a state of readiness.

I watched this happen with my son, Elisha, when he was only five years old. Since before our kids could properly talk, my wife and I made a habit of asking them at random times what they sensed God was saying to them at that moment. Most of the time their answer was somewhere between, "He loves me" to "He wants you to buy me a toy." The primary reason we did this was to have our kids used to the fact that God is always wanting to speak with them, and no matter where they're at or what they're doing, they have access to Him.

On one particular occasion, we were out at dinner when our waiter left to get our drinks, Elisha sat straight up and said, "Mom! God's speaking to me!"

"Well, what is He saying?" Erica responded.

"Well ... it's for the waiter."

Probing to make sure this was a legit word, she asked, "What does He want to say to the waiter?"

In a very matter-of-fact voice Elisha said, "Well, *He* wants *me* to tell him that he has a great voice, and he's not going to die!"

Stunned, Erica and I looked at each other and immediately started thinking of how we could deliver this word. So we decided to do what any responsible parent would do, we were going to make our kid do it.

Our waiter returned with our drinks, took our food order, and was about to walk away when I said, "Sir, one more thing. We're Christians and God speaks to us; my son has something he wants to tell you."

Intrigued this man looked at my son and walked over to his side of the table. He bent down to get to Elisha's level and said, "Now that's cute! What did God say?"

It was at this moment in our parenting experience that we found out our son had no volume control. Elisha put down his crayons, looked at the waiter, and shouted, "God says, 'You have a GREAT VOICE annnnddddd you're NOT GONNA DIIIIEEEEEE!'"

The waiter went from curious to crying in seconds and ran to the kitchen without saying a word to us. It didn't bother Elisha, who went right back to coloring, but I looked to my wife and said, "We have to leave. We need to leave now. Like right now!"

She shook her head at me, "No, we're staying here; let's see what happens."

To which I countered, "Babe, I know what's going to happen; they're going to spit in our food. We gotta go!"

Just then the waiter returned to our table and through broken sobs he managed to ask our son, "Okay! Okay! Tell me what He said one more time."

Elisha looked up at the crying waiter, annoyed that he had to stop coloring and repeated, "I said, God gave you a great voice, and you're NOT GONNA DIIIIIEEEE!"

The waiter is now weeping at our table. Sensing that this clearly meant something I asked, "Sir, does this make any sense to you?"

He had to regain his composure before telling us that he was pursuing a career in music and had some major opportunities open up for him. As all his hard work was about to pay off though, his father was killed in a car accident. Then a few weeks later his brother died the same way. Then a few weeks after that, his partner was also tragically killed in a car accident. After losing three loved ones in just months of each other, he assumed he was next and lived in constant fear of dying at any moment. He said it was so overwhelming, he couldn't sing to the best of his abilities and that all the doors that were once opened for his career became shut. He was so consumed by grief and fear that he wasn't able to sing anymore, so now the way he was paying his bills was by waiting tables.

I'm pretty sure my jaw dropped. I glanced at Elisha, and thought, "Not bad, bro. That's pretty accurate!" I looked at the waiter and asked if we could pray for him.

Looking at our whole family, he said, "Somebody needs to do something! Cause this is freaking me out right now!"

I called Elisha over to pray for this man since God made him the messenger. Elisha couldn't help but raise his voice one last time as he prayed, "God you have given him a great voice, and he's not going diiiiiiiiee!"

Now why would that happen? Because a five-year-old doesn't know normal. He sees everything with a different set of options because he carries heaven's perspective. Elisha knows that dangerous places are safe places in the Kingdom of God. We are raising him to walk in the ruined life and make sure he stays ready for when God calls on him.

Again, I believe you're reading this book because you desire the same thing. You are ready to risk it all and be a threat the enemy can take seriously. It's time for Heaven to consider you reliable and for hell to break into a cold sweat because you have chosen the ruined life. This book isn't in your hands to entertain you, but to enlist you. Welcome to your new normal!

THE GOD OF RIGHT NOW

I love verse 6, in Acts 3:6 because it forces us to make a choice—the "ruined life" or the "normal life." I love verse 6 because it carries power and authority with it. I also love verse 6 because the devil hates verse 6. The roar of excitement in Heaven must have hit record levels when they heard verse 6. Acts 3:6 reads:

> *"Then Peter said (to the beggar), 'Silver and gold I do not have, but what I do have I give you: In the name of Jesus Christ of Nazareth, rise up and walk'"* (Acts 3:**6**, context insert mine).

This beggar immediately received strength in his legs, stood up and walked into the temple with Peter. Peter's life is displaying what the Ruined Life looks like with every verse, but there is a crucial key demonstrated in verse 6. The ruined live with the reality that we serve the God of right now. Hebrews 13:8 gives us more context of this:

> *"Jesus Christ is the same yesterday, **today**, and forever."*

This makes it clear that Jesus doesn't change. Culture, circumstances, or opinions do not alter Who He is. This truth does come with a warning though. When Hebrews says, He is the same "yesterday, today, and forever," notice it starts off with "yesterday." This verse is describing the finished work of

Jesus Christ, but it also gives us insight to His character and reputation.

I cannot tell you how many times I've been caught up in the "yesterday" of God. When my pursuit of the ruined life points more to what Jesus has done through me in the past, instead of my present and future, I fight the sense of feeling stuck and unproductive. I've allowed my past breakthroughs to become trophies of comfort that weigh me down. I must remind myself He is the God of right now! "Yesterdays" are good to draw strength from as they remind us of what He's done, but we cannot live from them. It only makes us stale in our spirit and snobby to a fresh move of God.

However, there is a ditch on the other side of the road called, "forever" or we could call this "someday." When I would read the lives of the fathers and mothers of faith and revival, I caught myself saying, "*Someday,* I will walk in that authority. *Someday,* I will be that brand of risk-taker. *Someday,* I will cultivate that kind of lifestyle." Someday never came until I decided to be ruined and stopped avoiding the "dangerous places" He was creating right in front of me. I got tired of waiting for "someday" and started living with the truth that He is the God of right now!

The writer of Hebrews was limited to the language of his day and chose the word, "today," but this could be translated to our modern saying of "right now." This added perspective to my pursuit of the ruined life. When I see someone in crutches, I remind myself Jesus is the God of right now, and I lay hands on them. If I see someone hungry or broken, I serve the God of right now and watch as He uses me to bring food, courage, and hope.

I used to think in order to demonstrate power and love in dangerous places, I needed to be coming off a time of fasting or that I had to be on a certain "level" before I could see this happen in my life. That's just not true. When I rejected normal, I was ruined and started to pursue a lifestyle that required me to depend on Him being the God of right now. Truth is, Jesus can drop compassion on you for someone unexpectedly, and you don't have time to "spiritually prepare".

When you're ruined, you must remember He is the God of right now because in the real world, you don't get any prep time—people need what you have right now. The days of only making room for power in our services and conferences are over. God has always required this of us in our daily lives. Let it be said of your life, when God called on you, you were ready. You are ruined now. You have a new normal. Whether it's a psychic or a waiter or beggar—Jesus is the God of right now!

HOLINESS

As we continue to discover what the ruined life looks like, we must know what and Who our Source is. If we don't, we will end up flakey, or we'll be looking for encounters to validate our lifestyle. A true ruined life carries a consistent flow of love and power that can only come from a surrendered heart. Let's discover this together in the next chapter.

CHAPTER 3

INNER & OUTER ANOINTING

Thank you, Pastor Adam McCain for teaching and being a living example to many all over the world of what it is to have an Inner and Outer Anointing. I'm grateful to have a spiritual father like you, who nourished this in my life. Your words wrote this chapter.

My Pastor shared a story with me once about a guy named Steroid. It was competition weekend at Steroid's High School and during lunch, rival schools began to trash-talk each other. After fiercely going back and forth about who was the better school, they decided to settle things with an arm wrestling challenge. One school selected their strongest athlete and the other selected Steroid. I'm pretty sure you can imagine why!

With both schools crowding around one table, the challengers faced each other and locked arms. As soon as they heard the words "Go!" both began to use as much muscle as possible to crush their opponent and bring home the win. As the rival's tenacity increased, so did the roar from the crowd. There was more than just winning on the line. This was for bragging rights, and everyone knows those are priceless.

In the middle of the challenge, Steroid's focus on imposing his strength and dominating his opponent was at intense levels. He tightened his grip, pumped as much strength as he had left, and made his move. But all of sudden the bone in his forearm came shooting out of his arm. People quickly scattered as Steroid began screaming in pain. How could something like this happen? Steroid had muscles on top of muscles. Just by looking at him you could tell he was strong. So how could this have happened? Because the demand on Steroid's interior could not handle the demand on his exterior. He looked strong and capable on the outside, but was found to be weak and unsuited on the inside.

I can think of someone else that had a similar experience. His name was Sampson, and in Judges, chapter 13, Samson's parents encounter an angel who was there to announced his birth. Manoah, Samson's father asks a question which would be key in how his parents were supposed to raise him. Manoah asks, "What will be the boy's rule of life and work" (Judges 13:12). The angel would reply by instructing them to raise Sampson as a Nazarite. The Nazarites were extremely devoted in the service to the Lord by following the strictest code and manner of life. Samson was a Nazirite from birth, which meant he wasn't consecrated for a certain period of time; he was consecrated for his entire life to God. There's a lot expected of you when you are Nazirite, but Samson had to honor three standards specifically:

He could not go near or touch anything dead—This symbolized a separation from death which is the result of sin.

- He could not go near or touch anything dead—This symbolized a separation from death which is the result of sin.

- He could not shave the hair off of his head—This

showed he was under the authority of God, and God was his covering.

- He could not drink wine or touch grapes—This signified he had self-control by denying himself and not being under the influence of anything else but God.

Along with this Nazarite vow, Samson had unexplainable physical strength. From carrying city gates almost 40 miles (almost 60 km), to catching 330 foxes, tying them in pairs to a burning torch and setting them loose in his enemy's grain fields, to killing 1,000 men with only the jawbone of a donkey, this man was unstoppable. At least it looked that way until he slowly started to compromise his Nazarite vow, eventually breaking all of them.

First, he touched something that was dead while taking honey from a beehive that had grown in the carcass of the lion he killed just days before. (Judges 14:6-9; 15:15). This is so symbolic as sin may look sweet and enjoyable, but it is always surrounded by death.

Next, he drinks wine at his wedding to a Philistine woman, (when he was commanded only to marry an Israelite woman), and became so drunk that he makes a bet with the men from his wife's hometown that they cannot guess the answer to his riddle. These men threaten to kill Samson's new wife and her family if she doesn't tell them the answer. She begins to cry and manipulate Samson, until he finally gives her the answer. (Judges 14:10-20).

The Ruined need to notice how compromise works. When you put yourself in an environment or relationship where you think you can "walk the line," they will eventually wear you down until you are doing things you said you would never do. Samson later falls in love with a prostitute named Delilah, who would also manipulate him into revealing the secret to his strength was his hair.

It's interesting to note that Samson probably didn't look like a body builder. Because if he did, it would at least explain to everyone, including his enemies, where his "secret strength" (Judges 16:6) came from. He most likely had an average build and frame like many men in that day.

The Ruined must remember their secret strength comes from being under God's authority and covering. We're not strong because we're gifted or experienced, but because we are surrendered.

INNER & OUTER ANOINTING

Now here's why I relate Steroid and Samson together. Even while Samson was slowly breaking his Nazarite vows, he still had the ability to display great power and strength. Just like Steroid, he had the appearance of being untouchable and strong, but his interior was too weak to sustain the demand on his exterior. It's not about how much revelation you carry, how much power you demonstrate, or how much spiritual activity you have. Those "Outer Anointings" are worthless if you don't have a stronger "Inner Anointing."

Too many people are focused on displaying, while

ignoring the cracks in their foundation that will one-day cripple them. I've watched too many "anointed people" preach some of the most profound messages and carry a strong healing anointing, to only find their character was weak and their integrity was missing. Just like Steroid appeared strong in the middle of the moment and Samson was supernatural in the middle of being a pervert. We cannot afford to have a strong Outer Anointing while neglecting our Inner Anointing. The Ruined life does this in reverse. To understand this more, let's start putting some definition behind the terms, Outer Anointing and Inner Anointing.

OUTER ANOINTING

The Outer Anointing is your talent, skill, and gifting. People devote years, finances, and a tremendous amount of effort in developing these areas to be the best or to produce more because they want what they do to matter. I have found many develop their Outer Anointing because they're convinced they don't have one or they're not better than someone their comparing themselves to.

Romans 11:29 gives us some valuable insight. I want you to read it in several translations:

"For the gifts and the calling of God are irrevocable" (Romans 11:29).

"For God's gifts and his call can never be withdrawn" (Romans 11:29, NLT).

"God's gifts and God's call are under full warranty—never canceled, never rescinded" (Romans 11:29, The Message).

God's Word guarantees that we are all gifted in one thing or another. These gifts can never be taken or stolen away from you. You have no need to worry whether or not you are gifted, because the Word says you are. But you do decide whether you use your gifts, talents, and call for Kingdom purposes to bring glory and honor to Him. It's important to remember the discipline of sharpening your skill and craft is not a bad idea at all. We are called to be stewards and use our gifts well (1 Peter 4:10). However, sharpening your Outer Anointing at the neglect of your Inner Anointing is dangerous and unwise.

INNER ANOINTING

Your Inner Anointing is your character, integrity, and honor. These areas are vital to living The Ruined Life. Character refers to your moral and ethical qualities. Integrity refers to your ability to live by your moral and ethical qualities (or your character). Honor relates to our ability to show regard and reverence for God and others.

In my opinion, these areas are not celebrated enough, as they are not as easy to notice as our outward gifts and skills, but your Inner Anointing is the structure that holds your Outer Anointing in place. Peter says it like this:

*"His divine power has given us everything we need for a **godly life** through our knowledge of*

him who called us by his own glory and goodness.
Through these he has given us his very great and
precious promises, so that through them you may
*participate in the **divine nature,** having escaped*
the corruption in the world caused by evil
desires. For this very reason, make every effort
to add to your faith goodness; and to goodness,
knowledge; and to knowledge, self-control; and to
self-control, perseverance; and to perseverance,
godliness; and to godliness, mutual affection; and
to mutual affection, love. For if you possess these
*qualities in increasing measure, **they will keep***
you from being ineffective and unproductive
in your knowledge of our Lord Jesus Christ" (2
Peter 1:3-8, emphasis mine).

Peter encourages that we have been given every thing
we need to have a "godly life," "divine nature," or as we are
calling it an Inner Anointing. He boldly challenges us to cut no
corners when it comes to developing our Inner Anointing. Peter
even gives the ingredients of faith, goodness, knowledge, self-
control, perseverance, godliness, mutual affection, and love. All
of these can fall into the categories of character, integrity, and
honor:

CHARACTER: faith, goodness, perseverance, love

INTEGRITY: knowledge, self-control, love

HONOR: godliness, mutual affection, love

What's interesting also, is the sole purpose of the epistle of 2 Peter is to warn the Church of false leaders and teachers. In other words, people who have a strong Outer Anointing, but have no Inner Anointing. Why is this crucial to The Ruined? Because having an Inner Anointing will keep us from being "ineffective and unproductive" (2 Peter 3:8).

It is possible to be busy, showing off all of our talent, only for it to end up being fruitless. The neglect of an Inner Anointing is focusing more on how we look in public rather than who we are becoming in private. The Ruined must prioritize the cultivation of their Inner Anointing first; then, their Outer Anointing. It makes no sense to be so gifted, yet have no fruit to show for it.

The Ruined Life never causes you to be intoxicated and addicted with your Outer Anointing, but to be obsessed with developing your Inner Anointing. The Ruined give careful attention to how strong their character, integrity and honor is. At any moment, they sense a weakness in any one of these areas it is quickly prayed over, corrected, and brought into accountability. The Ruined know the Inner Anointing is the fuel for their Outer Anointing.

TO BE HONEST

I've watched in my own life that when I've leaned more on my Outer Anointing, I found I was becoming prideful and arrogant. I remember one time a mentor in my life heard a message I preached and caught an attitude rising inside of me.

It wasn't anything I said, but it was the tone and demeanor in how I delivered my message that caused them to challenge me.

I didn't realize it until later, but they were building my Inner Anointing. My wife is constantly asking, "How's your purity?" At first, I felt like I was being put under surveillance, but we have all seen too many traveling ministers who have fallen into scandal because this area wasn't kept accountable. She is helping me build my Inner Anointing.

Men I'm in covenant with are always reminding me to recognize when I'm vulnerable to temptation. Through the years they have taught me to *halt*. Whenever I am Hungry, Angry, Lonely or Tired, I need to H-A-L-T and get before the Lord or pick up the phone and call one of them. They are contributing to my Inner Anointing. My Pastor has taught me valuable boundaries, such as never being alone with the opposite sex, never touch God's money, and never trust your flesh or anyone else's. He's held me accountable to clean up any messes I have made and to be more focused on my marriage and family, while letting God build our ministry. He is helping me build a strong Inner Anointing.

I'm grateful for my wife, my family, and the leaders in my life who discern if my Inner Anointing is being neglected and address it quickly. At first, my pride made me believe they're not receiving my gift, and I should probably take it places where people will appreciate it. The truth was I was trying to avoid change and the reality that I was strong on the outside, but dry on the inside.

Looking back now, I see how their challenges to stop me

from focusing only on my Outer Anointing, while neglecting my Inner Anointing, actually brought great strength, power, and longevity to the call of God on my life. It was in these moments I discovered The Ruined Life is not about having moments of greatness, but a lifetime of greatness. This is why it's crucial to not neglect our Inner Anointing.

THE BASICS

The only way to build an indestructible Inner Anointing is to never ignore the basics. Psalm 11:3 says it best:

"If the foundations are destroyed,
What can the righteous do?"

The foundational, spiritual disciplines of reading the Word, developing a prayer life, fasting regularly, worshiping continuously, praying for the broken and sick, witnessing to the lost and hurting, is what keeps our heart aligned with His so we can avoid having compromise destroy us from the inside out. No one is ever above the basics, and when we think we are, it's a signal that we have a crack in our foundation.

The Inner Anointing can only be developed by the basics, and when I have started substituting the basics for Outer Anointing activity is when I found myself weak, exhausted, and vulnerable. There have been times when I've been busy with ministry and have become so dry, it's hard to discern the Spirit's leading.

In fact, I remember seasons where I had been so busy leading in ministry (Outer Anointing) that I was neglecting ministry (Inner Anointing), which only led me to be justify my busyness and neglect. I would make up excuses like, "Well, God knows my heart," or "If only He would send me more leaders to help carry the load." Can't tell you how many times I have said within myself, "When this season slows down, I'll be able to commit to my spiritual discipline again." How short-sighted I was being.

The Ruined make time with Him the highest priority of their life. Everything we will do that is worth anything and leaves a lasting impact flows from our relationship with Him (Acts 17:28). Busyness doesn't always mean effectiveness. I want to bring balance to this, also. There may be busy days that demand every minute you have. I remember when each one of my kids was born and the sleepless nights my wife and I would have or even during a busy season of hosting some of our conferences that go for consecutive weeks.

These days demand all your attention, but what I have learned is if I know there will be some disruption of my spiritual disciplines, I take extra time to be with Him in the days my time is being consumed. I feel a sustained awareness of His presence, and my heart stays fresh. Then, when I feel a longing start to develop, I prioritize my time, even at my own inconvenience, to pick up where I have left off. Busyness can numb our hearts and be so deceiving because we see fruit and impact coming from our Outer Anointing, but we must live from our hearts, sensitive to how our Inner Anointing is being developed. The Ruined never become familiar with the Basics.

ONLY ROOM FOR ONE

The Ruined Life is one full of risk and adventure, those pursuing it will see Super-natural demonstrations of love and power. Casting out devils, healing the sick, prophesying destiny, or even interpreting dreams will become common, but again there is a danger to it. As we are now familiar with the language, all those things are Outer Anointing centered. I love seeing displays like those, but they can be so intoxicating to the point that we live to see only those things. We start measuring our spiritual health and strength by them. We judge our services based on how "good" or "powerful" it was—if the preacher was on fire or not. We even base it on the response size during the altar call. If any of these or more were not to the level we desired, then we strive to find a way to get there, not realizing the strength of the Outer Anointing comes from the Inner Anointing.

The danger is we start living for this spiritual high and here is what's crazy—we can do it with zero Inner Anointing and a lot of charisma, skill, and talent. If we maintain this kind of "seeking the spiritual high" pattern, the crash afterwards is always ugly. Because when the service is over and you're back home and in your regular daily routine, there is only one of two things waiting for you. Your flesh or your spiritual discipline.

When you come off your spiritual high, these are the only two things waiting for you. If you have spent your time building your Outer Anointing, then your flesh is what you crash into. Have you ever noticed when you've come off a spiritual high, you end up irritable, insecure, or even falling into sin? That's because we've spent our time building our Outer Anointing and neglected our Inner Anointing.

Have you ever noticed a difference when you've been seeking Him consistently and hungering for Him daily, so that when you come off your spiritual high moment it doesn't drive you to your flesh, but to be with Him more. The moments that demand us to display our Outer Anointing should always lead us to build our Inner Anointing. We are all called to be encounter driven and desire spiritual gifts (1 Corinthians 14:1), but not as a substitute for our spiritual hunger.

Manifestations of God's love, freedom, and power are always an honor to be a part of, but encounters should not be what gives us our drive. We can have a strong Outer Anointing, but The Ruined need to remember there is a place for character, integrity, and honor. These being developed under the influence of the Holy Spirit will give you strengths such as wisdom, boldness, truth, authority, trustworthiness, morality, vision, and a secret history with God.

The Ruined live from their Inner Anointing and develop it through their spiritual hunger and discipline. Can you imagine how different Moses' relationship with the Lord would have looked, if he had kept looking for "burning bush encounters?" The Ruined must never live like this. Eventually, you will run out of bushes, (i.e. encounters, conferences, podcasts, and special anointings), and stay in your desert. Our hearts and life's focus must be on developing our spiritual hunger and disciplines. (If you're looking for a greater understanding on spiritual disciplines, I encourage you to take our Spiritual

Disciplines online course on www.chrisestrada.tv. It will give you insight and teach you daily habits to sustain both a strong Inner and Outer Anointing.)

HOLINESS

It crucial to cover the topic of holiness when it comes to the Inner and Outer Anointing. Truth is, I am shocked, not by what is being taught, but what's not being taught. It's rare to hear a message on holiness, and as someone who has raised leaders to pastor in the local Church, on a Bible college level, and even mentoring leaders from all over the world, the subject of holiness is vital.

There's two main reasons why we don't hear messages on holiness. One is the abuse of the message holiness as it has been taught without grace, which brings people to be legalistic. (You had to wear this type of clothing, you can only associate with certain types of people, etc.). This is obviously ridiculous because I could never work hard enough to be righteous and holy. I'm not righteous because of what I do. I'm righteous because of Who I know and put my faith in.

Staying true to the hermeneutic law of First Mention, in order to understand a principle or truth in the Bible, you need to find the first place the word is mentioned. The word righteousness is first mentioned in Genesis 15:6, after God makes His covenant with Abraham.

*"And he (Abraham) **believed in the Lord**, and He accounted it to him for **righteousness**"* (Genesis 15:6, emphasis mine).

64

Because Abraham believed God's covenant, God considered him righteous. In the same way, when we believe in the covenant, found in the finished work of Jesus, we can also become righteous. Paul writes in the book of Romans:

> *"This righteousness is given through faith in Jesus Christ to all who believe"* (Romans 3:22).

The second reason holiness is avoided being taught is it takes effort and surrender on our part. Many avoid preaching on holiness because they feel the Gospel will lose its appeal to the lost and hurting. But that is the beauty of holiness—to share with the lost and broken, who we were before we met Jesus and let them marvel at the transformation He has done in our life.

Again though, holiness taught without grace makes The Ruined Life look like a bunch of rules and lists of demands. Holiness that comes from the power of grace is what gives the Inner Anointing its core. Simply put, grace gives us the power to live holy, which is the epitome of the Inner Anointing. Pure grace gives us God's ability to live like Jesus and respond to life like He would.

My biggest frustration as a young believer was living holy. The constant failures and cycles of sin in my life would grieve my spirit. I repented constantly, and almost immediately after I hit a weak moment and fell into sin, but I always had a lingering sense of defeat. I'd repent, but do it again. Repent, but fall into the same sin. I remember feeling so discouraged. I believed I would never change. Yet this is how grace found me, and God showed me that I was repenting enough to be forgiven, but I wasn't surrendering enough to be changed.

You have to understand where I was at spiritually when I encountered grace. I had high spiritual activity (Outer Anointing), but I had shallow spiritual depth (Inner Anointing). I struggled to overcome habitual sin to lust, anger, and pride. Furthermore, when I ministered, my messages were focused mostly on God being demanding and harsh on those who couldn't keep godly standards. I was such a hypocrite! I became a zealot, and this pushed me to try harder, disciplining myself when I failed and beating myself up, so I learned to never do it again. How dumb!

Desperate for lasting change and knowing "will power" could not get me there, no matter how spiritual I became, is when I encountered the price and power of grace. The price of grace is surrender. The power of grace is freedom. Grace doesn't ask you to do everything, but it does ask you to surrender everything. The power of grace led to a consistency in my hunger for holiness that increased my Inner Anointing. I learned surrendering my decisions, future, pains, weaknesses and more, unlocked the power of Jesus to invade my life. The best part was it was effortless. When I surrendered, the ability to say "No" to sin and do the will of God became effortless. He was truly filling me with more of Himself, so I could live holy and right. This is why Peter writes:

> *"**Grace** and peace be multiplied to you in the knowledge of God and of Jesus our Lord, **as His divine power** (**What does he mean by "divine power?" GRACE!**) has given to us all things*

*that pertain to life and godliness, through the knowledge of Him who called us by glory and virtue, by which have been given to us exceedingly great and precious promises, that through these you may be partakers of the **divine nature*** **(How do we get the "divine nature?" By GRACE!)***, having escaped the corruption that is in the world through lust"* (1 Peter 1:2-4, emphasis mine).

Peter says through grace, Jesus' "divine power" was given so we could live holy and have an indestructible Inner Anointing, which then leads to having a "divine nature. In other words—a strong and balanced Outer Anointing! You could say grace and holiness are power twins! Inconsistency and weakness have no ground to stand on when grace arrives. Look at the Apostle Paul's secret weapon when dealing with his "thorn in the flesh,"

*"And He said to me, '**My grace** is sufficient for you, for **My strength** is made perfect in **weakness.**' Therefore most gladly I will rather boast in my infirmities, that **the power of Christ may rest upon me**. Therefore I take pleasure in infirmities, in reproaches, in needs, in persecutions, in distresses, for Christ's sake. For when I am weak, then I am strong"* (2 Corinthians 12:9).

Paul isn't relying on self-discipline and will power. He is counting on the unlimited source for a strong Inner and Outer

67

Anointing—Grace! You can take pleasure in hard times and weaknesses, because grace is going to make up for what you lack!

This is why it's dangerous to have a strong Outer Anointing, but neglect prioritizing the development of your Inner Anointing. If you think you can stay in a sinful lifestyle and then claim God's grace because you are spiritually active, friend, you don't know grace. You know a concept or principle of grace, but you haven't surrendered everything to receive grace.

When grace shows up in our lives it asks us to yield everything from our sin habits to low standards to our unforgiveness to our secrets. Grace is thorough because Jesus is thorough. So many people have misunderstood the work of grace when it begins to challenge us. The difference between the corrective work of grace and the paralyzing attack of condemnation is grace brings us to an awareness of conviction, whereas shame brings us to only a place of shame and guilt.

Don't get it twisted; grace will correct you because it's a work of love, and God only corrects the ones He loves (Hebrews 12:5, 6). But while He's correcting you and building your Inner Anointing, He is also building your Outer Anointing. Let me say it like this: The whole time you thought God was only bringing correction, He was also unveiling your greatness and destiny to you. This is why God can see the prophet inside of the pervert. The apostle inside of the addict. Destiny inside of the dysfunctional. He is so good! Let grace and holiness have its way, instead of getting in its way. I promise you won't regret it.

THE PROCESS

How do The Ruined sustain a lifestyle of developing our Inner Anointing? The Ruined must place a greater value on their Inner Anointing than their Outer Anointing. Focus less on building your gift (Outer Anointing), and commit more time and effort to building your identity (Inner Anointing). And when you become aware of a weak spot, here's a process you can use that will help you navigate your way to a place of grace, holiness, and strength.

1. IDENTIFY THE WEAK AREAS
    1 Corinthians 10:12 says, "Therefore let him who thinks he stands take heed lest he falls." If you're unsure about a weak area, ask those closest to you who will be honest with you and walk you through it. The biggest lie you'll ever believe is ignoring the fact that you don't have any weak areas. We all do!

2. PRAY VIOLENTLY
    I will always remember something Gordon Lindsay, the co-founder of Christ For The Nations, taught. He said, "Every Christian should pray one violent prayer a day!" If we are going to renew our spiritual vitality, we need to pray powerful prayers and not passive ones.

3. SURROUND YOURSELF WITH WISDOM & INTEGRITY
    Proverbs 11:3 says, "The integrity of the upright will

guide them." Wisdom is always found in a multitude of counselors. (Proverbs 11:4, 15:22, 24:6). Surrounding yourself with people who carry wisdom and integrity means it's bound to rub off on you. It's crucial to the process of developing a strong Inner Anointing.

4. YOU NEED TO GET IN THE WORD

Scripture is food for your spirit, which will nourish a weak area back to being a strong one. Paul reminds Timothy of this when he says, **"All Scripture** *is* given by inspiration of God, and *is* profitable for doctrine, for reproof, for correction, for instruction in righteousness, **that the man of God may be complete, thoroughly equipped for every good work"** (2 Timothy 3:16, 17). Getting into the Word will fill the cracks and fault lines that have created a weak area.

5. BECOME ACCOUNTABLE

James reminds us, "Confess your sins one to another, and pray for one another, so that you may be healed. The effective fervent prayer of a righteous man accomplishes much" (James 5:16). Confession about a weakness brings exposure to the issue. It allows grace to begin its work. There's a line in my wife's song, "Put On Your Brave" that says, "Confession breaks the obsession." So powerful and so true! Don't just stop at confession—ask for prayer. Prayer brings healing to the area of your heart and life that needs restoring. Again, almost repeating step 3—surround yourself with righteous people. People who are in right standing with God have an authority to accomplish more than those who are struggling in the same area you are. Nothing wrong with being around those who are fighting the same battle, but you need people who have authority in your life. Here's a simple test to know who truly has a place of authority in your life. If they can tell you "No" and you'll listen, or you're nervous about meeting with them about an issue, they have authority in your life.

This process has brought me through some of the hardest seasons of my life. When it was over, I realized I valued my Inner Anointing more. I've since noticed character, integrity, and honor continued to give me more fulfillment than the gifting on my life. The Ruined must remember it's the Inner Anointing that validates you, not the Outer Anointing. Both will satisfy, but only one is a source

PURSUIT

As we continue to pursue and develop The Ruined Life, there's a key ingredient The Ruined need to carry with them everywhere. Get ready to eat up the next chapter!

Chapter 4

HUNGER

The first time I ever went overseas was on a mission trip to Sri Lanka. I was 21, on my own, and ready to be a weapon in the Lord's hands. I preached almost every night during my three-week trip, so I was excited when I was invited to a believers' home for dinner and see the Sri Lankan way of life.

I remember they made this huge spread of food. Knowing they probably cooked more food for me than they probably ate in a month motivated me to eat whatever they put in front of me. Sri Lankan food is mostly rice and curry. I sat down at the table and the food kept coming. I had a mountain of rice mixed with beet curry, potato curry, chicken curry, eggplant curry, beef curry, carrot curry, and more. Then they gave me fruit salad, cookies, small cakes, all kinds of bananas, mangoes, and other fruit. In-between chewing, I chased all of this down with hot Coca-Cola, hot tea, and warm bottled water. None of it tasted bad, but I was stuffed.

I went to bed that night only to be awakened with some intense fellowship going on in my stomach. Has your stomach ever hurt so badly at night that you lay on your side and that gives you relief? But then, all the food you ate collects on that side, thus beginning to hurt your stomach again. So you quickly switch to lay over on your other side, only to sense the same process begins to repeat itself all over again. You end up tossing and turning, trying to sleep or worse, you end like I did, spending all night on the toilet.

Anyone who has been through this before knows it's a waste of time because that part of the anatomy is out of order by this time! Not sleeping at all that night wasn't how I wanted to start the next day. I was taking a train from Kandy to Colombo and the pastor I was with suggested we take the first class car that had "air conditioning." First class wasn't the best idea, either, as it was a train car surrounded with glass windows and their version of air conditioning was a desk fan with a rotating head, bolted to the ceiling.

Sri Lanka has some intense jungle heat, so to be in a glass box with a desk fan barely blowing on you and an upset stomach that feels like it has 27 demons in it is a recipe for a great way to start this chapter! The train started to depart, and it shook side to side, which caused my stomach to turn immediately. After 20 minutes of try to beast it, I decided, "Enough! I'm going to force myself to throw up off of this train."

I opened my car door only to find the section between train cars was jammed packed with people. But I was determined and finally made my way to the bathroom. Until this point in my life, I never knew I could be picky about where I vomited, but when I looked at this toilet, it was a firm, "No!" The toilet was made of just a seat and a plastic pipe that had the remains of everyone that had gone before me. I stood in shock at the condition of this restroom as I could see the train track at the end of the pipe. I quickly threw open the door and came to terms with my only other option. Open the entire train car door and puke off the side of the train.

I could hear the confusion in the voices of all the people who felt the strong wind rush through the cart section, when they saw this sweaty American sitting off the side in the delivery position, (think of a woman in labor, but giving birth to a T-Rex—that's what my faced looked like). I knew the only way to bring relief to my innards was to throw up. I stuck my finger down my throat, and here it came. Oh, the relief and feeling of freedom I experienced—priceless, just priceless.

The conversations behind me went into hysteria, but I just took it as crowd support and tried to puke even harder, so the crowd could appreciate my dominating performance. But then I realized what they were yelling about. As I was puking, I didn't realize there were people who had their window down and my vomit was getting all over them. It was too late now, once you start, you can't stop, so I kept vomiting.

Then, out of nowhere, I see a guy under me. I felt the earth's rotation slow down; time came to a crawl as I made eye contact with my next victim. As we locked gazes, a fresh gush of yellow-orange puke came rushing out of my mouth. It was almost like it had a mind of its own, wanting to hug this man and crash onto his face and chest. But then, there was another guy. And then another guy. And another one. I didn't realize they were building another track on the other side. I must have sprayed like 20 workers as the train rushed by.

To this day, I still feel bad for all the people I baptized, but the sense of relief I had afterwards was worth it (I know how bad that sounds, but it's my ugly honesty). As I got up from where I was sitting, all the people behind me had their jaws dropped, and I closed the door with the look of "That's how it's done!" I went back to my chair to enjoy the rest of my train ride. Yes, this is a true story. My life is one insane event after another. I've been ruined and wouldn't want it any other way.

Looking back, what I would have liked was for someone to have told me what I should have eaten and what I should not have eaten. I wish someone would have said, "Chris, if you eat that, you will pay for it later." If only someone with some experience was there to caution me. Isn't the same true when it comes to situations in our life? Don't you wish someone would have told you, "You don't want to date them?" Or even, "You want to avoid clicking on that, because that will quickly turn into an addition you don't want to bring into your marriage."

With so many opportunities and temptations to feed yourself, it is pivotal for us to guard our hunger! The worst thing that could happen to The Ruined is they allow the enemy to sabotage their appetite. Why? Because if the enemy can get your hunger, he can control the amount of courage, strength, and impact that flows off of your life.

It's interesting that the first time hunger is mentioned in the Bible is in Genesis 2:16 when God says, "You are free to eat." That promise is true to this day. You and I can choose to hunger for Him or to hunger for the things of this world and the flesh. There is a natural and spiritual law that exists today which says, "What you feed on is what you will hunger for and release in your life." If you feed on negativity, you will hunger for it and release it. If you feed on perversion, you will hunger for it and release it. If you feed on life, you will hunger for it and release it. If you hunger for Jesus, you will hunger for and release Him everywhere you go. We must remember we hunger for what we feed on and need to fuel ourselves correctly.

INTENTIONAL HUNGER

If we are going to remain "ruined," then we need to be purposeful with how we feed and satisfy ourselves. My wife and I have four kids, we love very much. Which means, she has told me she was pregnant four times, but surprised me four different ways of sharing the news with me. One thing stayed the same each time she told me, and that was the face she would make. Let me bring some definition to this.

When she told me she was pregnant with our oldest Elisha, I had literally just stepped off the bus from a week long mission trip to the Navajo Reservations of Arizona. I was tired and hungry, but excited to see my wife. We got into our car to drive home, and as I put my hand on the transmission to reverse, she put her hand on mine and gave me "that look."

The white around her brown eyes got bigger, her eyebrows seemed to be peaking, while she smiled with no teeth just a sharp lip line. Her facial expression was doing all of this, but she didn't say anything. To me this "look" does not say, "Guess what? I'm pregnant!" What it says to me is, "Hi! I'm a serial killer." I doubt that if you were in the car, too, you could have read her face and concluded Erica was pregnant.

So as she gave me this look, I replied with, "I missed you too honey." But then she took my hand and placed it on her stomach while maintaining the same face. I felt like it all fell into place for me right then, and thought, "Oh, that's why she's looking at me like that. She's hungry." So I told Erica, "I'm hungry too, babe; let's go get something to eat."

I realized I wasn't understanding what she was saying with her look because she began to cry. Erica intensified the look, which only made me more confused, which caused her to look even more like a serial killer. I remember thinking, "I'm the world's worst husband because all I did was come home, and with her not saying anything, I made her cry!

So being the clueless husband I was, I said, "Honey, I'll let you pick the restaurant." My wife is amazingly patient with me, especially when I'm struggling with the spirit of stupid. She then took my hand and pressed it harder against her stomach, but still giving me the, "I'm one of America's Most Wanted look." I'm pretty sure heaven intervened because right then all the dots connected. I responded with one word—"Oh! Oooohhhhh! Oh, oh, OH! Ooooooooohhhhh!"

Every time my wife told me she was pregnant, she always made "that face." Even with the fourth child, I never read it immediately, but I did catch on a lot faster.

One other thing I noticed that was consistent with my wife was how she cared for our children, while she was pregnant. Pregnancy demands a lot of a woman, but one key area it changes is a woman's appetite. Erica has always been a very clean eater, but she was overly intentional with how she ate, so she could nourish our unborn children properly. She would choose to eat certain fruits and vegetables that were not a part of her normal meal, because she knew that doing so would make our baby strong and healthy. I was impressed with how she willingly changed what she took in, because she knew it was her responsibility to care for what she carried. She was feeding herself correctly. Always directing her cravings toward the ultimate goal of delivering a healthy baby.

I liken this to the Ruined Life. We must realize what we carry—inner anointing, destiny, revival, authority, etc.—needs to be fed correctly. Spiritual cravings don't just happen; they are developed by feeding them. What type of spiritual appetite and cravings are you creating? Is what you're carrying being nourished correctly so you can sustain the Ruined Life? Remember, you will hunger for what you feed on.

The main reason we eat is to fuel ourselves to make the most out of our day. The main reason we need to feed our spiritual appetites is so we can fuel ourselves so that God can make the most out of our lives. I'm guilty of my fair share of missed moments of spiritual meals, but it's then I must remember it is my job to feed myself. I must be intentional with my hunger for Him. If I'm not eating, then that means I'm starving myself. If I make a habit out of that, I will not last and will burnout, or worse, fall away from Him.

When I don't eat in the natural, my body screams it's hungry, but in the spiritual when I don't eat, the opposite occurs. My spirit gets quieter, and I find it increasingly difficult to sense His direction for my life or even what He is saying as I minister to people. If I don't feed my spirit often, I will end up being unfamiliar with His voice and miss moments because I was malnourished and unable to recognize His presence. Don't allow your spirit to get dull and numb. Feed yourself correctly!

Your spiritual hunger is your spiritual thermometer, and it will never lie. I have been convicted many times when I feel spiritually starved, but find a way to make time for things that have no eternal value. Please, don't be legalistic when you read that. Understand that God desires for you to enjoy your life and wants you to fill it with passions and hobbies, but those should never replace your appetite for Him.

What God blesses as an additive, He will curse as a supplement. We must never be the type of people who only eat when there's a church service. We must be known by our hunger for Him, instead of starving ourselves with only a once-a-week meal, and that's if we go to church. We must have the spiritual discipline of consistency when it comes to our time in His Word and our prayer lives.

Think of it like this. When someone is sick, the first thing to go is their hunger, then their strength, and eventually their body starts shutting down. The same is true with your spirit man. Spiritual sickness or dryness starts when we lose our appetite, then our faith, grace, and strength to fulfill the Lord's direction for our life begin to diminish until our spiritual life feels dry, stale, and powerless.

The Ruined must never allow their spirit to grow dull and lose their hunger for Him. We must be intentional to feed our spirit intentionally.

SPIRITUAL HUNGER IS MY RESPONSIBILITY

By now I'm sure you can see why spiritual hunger is our own personal responsibility, but I would like to bring more insight to this. I find a great truth in Proverbs 27:7 when it says, *"The satisfied soul loathes the honey-comb."*

What this means is that when we fill our lives with "other things," even when God's sweet presence comes (the honey-comb), we will not want it, or we won't have room in our lives for Him. Are we busy satisfying ourselves off of other things that do not matter or are we stuffed with the world, loaded down with worldly desires and passions? Maybe we have enough "spiritual activity" in our lives to fool others, even ourselves, to look like we want Him, when really we don't have any room.

When we are loaded down with the things of the world, we may not be rejecting Him, but we will be disinterested in Him. Stop satisfying yourself with worldly things and start increasing your spiritual hunger. It is not God's job to increase our hunger for Him. It is our spiritual responsibility to increase our hunger for Him.

We must keep away from worldly sources and pleasures that pollute our heart. The word "worldly" or "world" in the Bible refers to either a broken system or broken humanity. You see "world or worldly" living and thinking, addressed many times throughout the Scriptures. It's only capable of leading people to weakness and immaturity (1 Corinthians 3:1-3, 18-19, 2 Corinthians 7:10, James 4:4, Ephesians 4:14-15, 1 John 5:19, John 16:33). The Ruined should never draw from a source that leaves us broken, but from Him Who will keep us whole and healthy. The pure pleasures of this world are permitted in our life, but if we over eat, we will find ourselves imbalanced and making up excuses for why the Lord lets us, "get away with it."

Eventually, we will find we have nothing in our tank and begin to feel distant from Him. I want to plead with The Ruined; never allow yourself to get to this place, and if you do, I encourage you to do whatever it takes to build your spiritual appetite back up.

BECOMING FAMILIAR WITH HIS VOICE

I have found myself spiritually frustrated more times than I care to remember. Early on in my prayer life, I would experience seasons of hearing God's voice with such clarity, it was encouraging and life-giving. But just when I found myself familiar with His voice, He would go silent. At first, I examined my heart to see if I had done anything to offend or grieve Him, but I felt no sense of conviction.

The only thing I knew to do was to continue with my spiritual discipline and keep waking up in the morning to meet with Him. Those mornings were so dry, and I felt like my prayers wouldn't make it past my ceiling in my living room. Until finally, I would hear Him whisper and sense how it reinvigorated my soul and brought life to my spirit. Then the next few days the volume of His voice would increase and revelation would begin to flood my heart. Until eventually, I felt like He was shouting in my spirit to where I couldn't journal fast enough and become so overwhelmed, I would just cry as tears of gratefulness poured down the sides of my face.

However, the cycle would repeat itself, and I would sense He went "silent" again. I examined my heart again, only to find that nothing was wrong. So I did what I knew to do and that was to stay loyal to being in His Word and presence. Sure enough, I would hear His whisper, then the volume would increase until it became a shout in my spirit.

I'm sure many are reading this and saying, "I've been so frustrated, because I'm experiencing the same thing. Many ask, "Why does God go silent on me sometimes? Is He ignoring me?" Never! What God is trying to do is create a greater hunger on the inside of you. He is increasing your ability to be familiar with His voice. If I was alone in a room with Erica, I could make out her voice because we were by ourselves. Imagine if I was in a conference room with her and other people; it would take some time to hone my hearing to her voice, but eventually I would be able to make out her voice in that setting.

Let's say I was in a shopping mall during Christmas, and I was listening for her voice. Again, it would take some time, and my ability to make out her voice alone would be tested; but believe it or not, I can now make out her voice in a crowded mall. The same is true with the Lord.

Your growth causes your spiritual sensitivity to grow, and your ability to hear His voice increases. But the Lord desires greater and deeper intimacy with us, which is why when we have found our rhythm at journey point with the Lord, He goes "silent." He wants you to pursue greater and deeper intimacy with Him. Then when His whisper becomes a shout, He will repeat the process. He is never ignoring us, but often He is waiting on us.

I know many of you reading this desire greater intimacy with the Holy Spirit, and I would like to invite you to utilize our online course called, "Hearing The Voice of God." This will help give even more insight and habits in developing clarity in hearing His voice and sensing His leading. You can find out more at www.chrisestrada.tv.

SPEAK, LORD; YOUR SERVANT HEARS

A constant prayer of mine is for an army of Samuels to rise and to become familiar with His voice as early as possible in their life. How dangerous could a generation become to the enemy if they become devoted to the leading of His voice? What dreams would be given to them in their preteen years? What nations would they be shaking in their twenties? What churches would they be building in the thirties and forties? What kind of leaders would they be releasing into every arena throughout their entire lives? Just dreaming about it stirs my heart.

If you remember, Samuel begins to hear God at a young age, but doesn't recognize it is God (1 Samuel 3). He actually thinks it is Eli, the High Priest, as Samuel was under his mentorship at the time. The fact is crystal clear. Samuel was young, and he began to hear the Lord call to him at a young age.

It's important we all understand that age doesn't decide our hunger level. Remember, Samuel is a young boy when he begins to hear the voice of the Lord. I believe children actually do hear the voice of the Lord, but don't know it because they haven't had anyone train them to recognize His voice.

As a parent, the greatest impartation and legacy I can leave to my kids is to recognize the voice of God in their life and to be led by it. I am amazed when one of my kids comes to Erica or me and shares something they dreamed, heard, or sensed the Lord whispered to them. It feels like an answer to our prayers, but there is a continued urgency to pursue Him more.

I think it is worth referencing that after the first time Samuel heard the Lord call to him, but didn't recognize God's voice, that he didn't try to go above and beyond to get his attention the second time He called him. Why? Because God was developing a greater hunger and extending the invitation to Samuel to become familiar with His voice.

Take heart in this as you build your hunger for Him. Searching the heart of God and familiarizing yourself with His voice is a unique journey for everyone. Very few will look alike, but all end up with the same thing—a passionate desire for Him that is never satisfied.

It should comfort us to a degree that Samuel didn't recognize His voice at first, either, but we should also feel provoked. In the end, he eventually became so familiar with the Lord's voice that all of Samuel's prophetic words came to pass (1 Samuel 3:19).

I believe that all started with the cry that began Samuel's journey for clarity and intimacy. Samuel responded to the Lord with, "Speak, Lord, for your servant hears." This ruins me every time, because Holy Spirit is always searching for hearts to respond in the same way when His "sweet honeycomb" passes by their life. We must be diligent to respond when He initiates, and we must be devoted to growing our hunger and drawing near to Him (James 4:8). Reserve your greatest hunger for Him!

To the degree you fill yourself with Him is the degree you will respond to Him. When we stop trying to satisfy ourselves off of social media, TV, sports, or anything else, we will be led to some of the greatest moments of our lives. The Ruined Life is where salvations, signs, wonders, healings, and miracles become normal, and we must be well equipped with our greatest weapon—the Voice of the Living God. In the next chapter, it will prove to be the foundation for the Ruined to release revival.

Chapter 5

TREASURE HUNT TRAINING

I'm in airports all the time. (Fun fact, I'm waiting for a flight in LAX right now as I write this). I love to people watch. One of my favorite things to watch is how family and friends reunite at the airport. In my people watching, I have noticed there is a difference between the way women and men greet each other after they've been away for some time or as short as weekend.

Ladies, if your girl comes back from being gone for just the weekend, it's a rule to bring balloons, flowers, chocolates, and signs in multiple colors, complete with sequins and glitter. And that's the minimum. When you finally see them come out of the exit, I have witnessed record-setting, high pitch squeals come out of you, as you run with your hands up to throw around their neck, and begin to admit you didn't know what to do with your life while they were gone. You immediately inquire of them to tell you every detail of their trip, starting with what they wore, ate, and did, while you're waiting for their luggage. You even paid the extra money to park first row to get to the car fast enough to get them quickly to the surprise party you've planned.

Guys are a lot different. We don't do signs, flowers, balloons, and chocolates. We don't get out of the car to meet you once you exit to baggage claim. We circle around the arrivals lane at the airport and tell you to text, once you got your luggage. Then, we'll pull right up to the curb. Only really good friends help you put your luggage in. Otherwise, we pop the trunk and make you do it. Once in the car, we're not expecting a detailed report. The most exciting the conversation gets goes like this:

"How was it?"

"Good."

"That's cool."

Seriously, that's about it.

One of my favorite types of reunions to watch is when kids run up to their parents when they come out of the exit at the airport. The parent intensely scans the crowd looking for their little one. The kids always spot the parents first and tear through the crowd like a cheetah in the bush of Africa, screaming Daddy or Mommy all the way up to them. I witnessed this one time when I arrived in Atlanta fresh off a red-eye flight, completely jet lagged and thinking I had landed home in Dallas. I was missing my wife and kids a lot, as I was on an extended trip, when two kids came running through the crowd in the same fashion I described above.

Instinctively I knelt down with my arms open ready to be half tackled while scooping them up and squeezing them tight. But the closer they got the less excited they became. When they came into reach, I moved to grab them, when suddenly they went right around me and hugged the man behind me. I just made myself look like a fool, and I'm sure the Dad behind me was wondering why I was trying to scoop up his kids. So, I played it off as smoothly as I could think of in the moment. I pretended to tie my shoe as I was kneeling down.

Treasure hunting is similar, as we are looking to reunite people with their Heavenly Father. The kids I was trying to hug knew I wasn't their father, which is why the expression on their face changed—I was an unconvincing substitute.

Hurting and broken people are desperate to find life, healing, and freedom that only comes through Jesus Christ. And we will be offering no substitutes. It's time to reunite people with their Heavenly Father, and we have to be a vehicle for that encounter to happen.

This is the heart behind "treasure hunting." Treasure Hunting is a strategy using words of knowledge, Spirit-led instincts, and super-natural boldness to demonstrate the love and power of God. Treasure Hunting is not an event, but a lifestyle that The Ruined must sustain so we can stay sharp and ready.

To understand the strategy of Treasure Hunts better, let's look at Acts, chapter 9 Saul of Tarsus, who would become the Apostle Paul, is on his way to Damascus to arrest, if not kill, Christians. On his way there, he encounters Jesus and becomes ruined for the rest of his life! He becomes temporarily blind after this powerful encounter and is led into Damascus until an unexpected visitor shows up. Acts, chapter 9 reads:

> *"Now there was a certain disciple at Damascus named Ananias; and to him the Lord said in a vision, 'Ananias.' And he said, 'Here I am, Lord.' So the Lord said to him, 'Arise and go to the street called Straight, and inquire at the house of Judas*

for one called Saul of Tarsus, for behold, he is praying. And in a vision he has seen a man named Ananias coming in and putting his hand on him, so that he might receive his sight.' Then Ananias answered, 'Lord, I have heard from many about this man, how much harm he has done to Your saints in Jerusalem. And here he has authority from the chief priests to bind all who call on Your name.' But the Lord said to him, 'Go for he is a chosen vessel of Mine to bear My name before Gentiles, kings, and the children of Israel. For I will show him how many things he must suffer for My name's sake.' And Ananias went his way and entered the house; and laying his hands on him he said, 'Brother Saul, the Lord Jesus, who appeared to you on the road as you came, has sent me that you may receive your sight and be filled with the Holy Spirit.' Immediately there fell from his eyes, something like scales, and he received his sight at once; and he arose and was baptized.' So when he had received food, he was strengthened. Then Saul spent some days with the disciples at Damascus. Immediately he preached the Christ in the synagogues, that He is the Son of God" (Acts 9:10-20).

YOUR "AVERAGE" BELIEVER

Let's highlight several keys in this passage. First, I love that Ananias is never titled as an Apostle, Prophet, Teacher, Pastor or Evangelist. All we know is he is a believer, who had a spiritual discipline of prayer and received instructions from the Lord one day. You don't need a title when God places a purpose on your life. These types of assignments are not just for the "spiritual elite," but for all believers to have this kind of a lifestyle.

CLUES

Next, notice what gift of the Spirit Ananias is operating in here. It is the gift of Words of Knowledge (1 Corinthians 12:8). Words of Knowledge is when a believer knows information about a person or situation that they could not have naturally assumed or concluded. They were given this information supernaturally by the power of the Holy Spirit. God gave spiritual gifts to believers so we could minister effectively with authority and power, and we must use them often (1 Corinthians 12:4-11).

Words of knowledge behave like clues that lead us to an encounter and helps us minister effectively when we come across a person or situation. We know this gift is in operation by the "clues" Ananias is being given:

- Go to the street called "Straight"

- Inquire for the house of Judas for one called "Saul of Tarsus"

- He has seen you coming in a vision
- When you put your hands on him, he will receive his sight.

These are all "clues" that lead to Saul receiving his sight back. The same is true for how the Ruined will operate. God will lead you by words of knowledge/clues, which will direct you to people and situations that need hope, healing, encouragement, or salvation. People are treasures to God, and we are his "treasure hunters," willing to be used by God so He can show His love and power to them.

PRESENTATION - DEMONSTRATION = ABOMINATION

The Ruined understand it is our responsibility to present the gospel of Jesus Christ and to demonstrate it at the same time. I like to say it like this, Presentation without Demonstration is an Abomination! It's not enough to just share a good message, especially in today's culture. They are used to that. We live in a day and age where the Gospel Message is accessible and it's everywhere. If people wanted to hear our messages, we have plenty of books, podcasts, YouTube channels, TV and radio stations, social media accounts and more for them to hear it.

We have all of this, but we're still not transforming cities. If presenting the message was all it took to win the masses, then how come we haven't taken whole nations? Because we are not to just present the love and power of God, but to demonstrate it! Please understand my heart. I am not being cynical of the Church. I love the Church! Nor am I being cynical of certain styles of ministering. But presenting the gospel of Jesus Christ and demonstrating the power of it is a biblical truth. We have incredible communicators and preachers who can word-smith great messages, but they are weak in altar calls and demonstrating the power of God. And that's at church! If we're not seeing it in our church services, then I'm pretty sure it's non-existent in the daily lives of believers. It shouldn't be this way.

It's harsh, but true, that people are bored with our messages because they've heard them all before. This is why many have dismissed this younger generation as spiritually lazy, numb, and lethargic. I don't believe they are any of those things. I believe they are just bored because the Christianity we've been showing them is so boring. But when broken arms start to get healed and the dead start to be resurrected, Christianity is no longer boring. It's an adventure that will ruin you for the rest of your life.

I've watched as churches and student ministries have resorted to gimmicks and giveaways to pack out their services. I have always taught our staff and leaders, what we catch people on, we have to keep them on. If I'm catching them on giving away flat screen TVs, PlayStations, and vacations, as soon as I stop or another church adopts the same strategy, they'll be leaving fast. I've watched too many blow through budgets, but have very little growth. Their services were packed, but the impact was little-to-none.

We are living in a day that is opposite to what we read in Peter's words in Acts 3:6 when he says, "Silver and gold I do not have, but what I do have I'll give you. In the name of Jesus Christ of Nazareth rise up and walk."

We now have plenty of silver and gold, but what we don't have enough of is the power of God! It's expensive to be powerless! But when you catch them on the love of God and the power of the Holy Spirit, they'll stay regardless of the "perks." I'm all for fresh methods and strategies, but I'm not okay with it serving as a replacement for presentation and demonstration. When these two are used together consistently, peoples' lives will be transformed forever. Even Paul had to remind the church at Corinth of this non-negotiable truth.

> *"And I, brethren, when I came to you, **did not come with excellence of speech or of wisdom** declaring to you the testimony of God. For I determined not to know anything among you except Jesus Christ and Him crucified. I was with you in weakness, in fear, and in much trembling. And **my speech and my preaching were not with persuasive words of human wisdom, but in demonstration of the Spirit and of power**, that your faith should not be in the wisdom of men but in the power of God"* (Acts 2:1-5).

It wasn't Paul's polished preaching that turned their hearts to the Lord; it was his preaching and his demonstration of the "Spirit and power." I believe we should have captivating sermons and unforgettable illustrations, peppered all throughout our messages, but even then, it is never a substitute for the power of God. I declare to you, The Ruined, that altars will be packed and those in your circle of influence will respond, when we start to present and demonstrate the love and power of God regularly!

LORD, YOU SURE?

All of us can relate to Ananias when he says, "Lord, I have heard from many about this man; how much harm he has done to Your saints in Jerusalem. And here he has authority from the chief priests to bind all who call on Your name."

That's another way of saying, "God, you sure? Wait, You want me to do what for who?" What Ananias is about to learn is what the Ruined always remember—don't be surprised if the Lord asks you to go behind enemy lines. He is in the habit of requesting this from us often.

Ask Gideon. (Judges 7). God whittles Gideon's army 32,000 to 300. The night before the battle, God comes to Gideon, already knowing he is scared out of his mind, and says to Gideon, "If you are afraid, go down to the camp with Purah your servant, and you shall hear what they say; and afterward your hands shall be strengthened to go down against the camp" (Judges 7:10).

God is literally telling Gideon to go into his enemy's camp and God will encourage him there; then he will walk away with an assurance of victory. Gideon goes and overhears a dream that has spread throughout the camp, and the interpretation has been made that it can only mean one thing—Gideon and his army are going to destroy all of them. Gideon now realizes that not only is he guaranteed the victory because God said he would have it, but he is being filled with strength and courage to dominate on the battlefield. Gideon is getting encouraged in his enemy's camp. The same will be true for the Ruined.

Don't be surprised when God asks you to go behind enemy lines. God loves a good ambush, and the Ruined should never lose their ability to be a surprise attack for the Kingdom of God. We should never let our lives become spiritually predictable when it comes to being used by God. What makes the Ruined dangerous for good is they are just as unpredictable as the God they serve.

GO

This key is simple, but true. God's response to Ananias, confirming what he heard from the Lord, started with the word "Go." I have learned a secret. God is with those who "go." He starts the great commission with "Go" (Matthew 28:19, 20). This command of "go" separates the men from the boys and the women from the girls. This has to be one of his favorite words, for many reasons, but one of the simplest is, when we choose to "go," it shows a complete dependence on Him. People who live like this have His undivided attention and will be supplied with everything they need to carry out their assignment. Why? Because He can trust them at a moments notice and a deeper level. The Ruined live for hearing the Lord say to them, "Go!"

"onGOing"

As Ananias submits to the leading of the Holy Spirit, it's important to notice he still had some questions he needed God to answer. God doesn't mind you having questions, as long as you are "going" while you're asking. We know this is the case, because the first time the Holy Spirit gave him words of knowledge/clues, it was also the directions about where to go, who to look for, and what they need prayer for. But there had to be some "onGOing" conversation, because when Ananias showed up, he knows details about what happened to Saul, even though he wasn't with him when it happened. Acts 9:17 says:

> *"Brother Saul, **the Lord Jesus, who appeared to you on the road as you came**, has sent me that you may receive your sight and be filled with the Holy Spirit."*

How did Ananias know the Lord appeared to him on the road he travelled, unless he had an ongoing conversation with Jesus about Saul? Again, Jesus doesn't mind you asking questions and pressing in for more details, as long as you are going. God can't use someone greatly, if you're needing Him to supply every detail before you make the decision to "go." It's important for The Ruined to realize that God will add to your details as you are going or even when you have "found" who He sent you to. Almost every time I find who He sent me to, either while I'm looking or while I'm praying for them, He almost always adds more to the message and ministry I'm delivering. Never be hesitant to have "onGOing" conversations with Him.

EXPECT SALVATIONS, SIGNS, WONDERS, HEALINGS, & MIRACLES

"Immediately there fell from his eyes, something like scales, and he received his sight at once; and he arose and was baptized" (Acts 9:18).

As soon as Ananias prayed for Saul to receive his sight, the results were instant because the authority for miracles was made available. When you are given Words of Knowledge/ Clues, expect for the power of God to be released when you find your treasure/person. Nothing proves the love of God more than when miracle-working power is demonstrated. You can debate and try to convince people all day long, but nothing is more convincing to the broken and hurting than when they see God do a miracle in their life. It's what sets us apart from all the other "messages" out there.

Always remember, if people can be argued into it, they can be argued out of it, as well. But when they hear the message and see it demonstrated, it doesn't matter how convincing the argument is, it will be tested by if it produced the raw power of God in their life.

It would be a great act of negligence if I didn't address an important issue The Ruined need to remember, as they develop this lifestyle. Everyone loves a good miracle story. We love hearing the reports of the dead rising and cancer disappearing. I thank God for all of this, but we must be careful not to over celebrate these testimonies and look at the ones that have less 'wow factor' with familiarity. The person you are sent to may not have stage 4 cancer, but they might be struggling with guilt because they think they're not a good parent.

I remember when I was at a fast food, drive through window, and my daughter, Jasmine, got a clue for the women helping us. I rolled down the back seat window, and my daughter simply told her, "Jesus told me to tell you, 'you're a good mommy, and you should never doubt that.'" Awe-struck turned to tears in seconds, and she ran off without giving us our food. (It is a great tension in my life, but sometimes when all you want to do is have lunch, God wants to have revival. Ha! We can't have both, sometimes).

The manager quickly came to the window and asked if everything was okay with our order. I told him everything was fine, so he asked, "Why did she run off like that?" I did what any parent would do in this situation; I made Jasmine explain to the manager what just happened. Confidently, Jasmine said, "Don't worry, Jesus just wanted to remind her she is a good mommy."

Shocked by her answer, the women returned and said to Jasmine, "You don't know how much I needed to hear that. Just this morning I was beating myself up for having to drop my kids off earlier than all the other kids at school in order to make it to one of my three jobs. I told myself I was a failure as a mother because I'm a single parent with three kids, and I have to work all the time. I wish we spent more time together, but

I have to have these three jobs because it's the only way I can pay my bills. But then you show up and tell me what I needed to hear. Thank you!"

Please notice, nobody's tumor fell on the floor, but a woman received the miracle of encouragement, and to her, that was just as powerful as someone rising from the dead.

Everyone wants the "suddenly" stories in their life, but in order to get the suddenly, you have to do the subtle really well. Don't only celebrate the "Grand Dios" moments, but celebrate every time He uses you—no matter what He uses you for. Then, you can be trusted with the "suddenly."

YOU DON'T KNOW

Ananias was aware of Saul's reputation and was given a glimpse into how the Lord would use him for the rest of his life, but I don't think he realized who he was ministering to. All Ananias knew was he was being sent to someone who could legally murder him. He didn't realize this would be the man who would write two thirds of the New Testament. He had no idea Saul of Tarsus would become the Apostle Paul. He probably was completely unaware this man would give the revelation to the Church, that we are a "new creation in Christ Jesus. Behold all things have passed away and all things have become new." (2 Corinthians 5:17).

(SIDE NOTE: If you are wanting to discover who you are and what your life's purpose is then I encourage you to go through our online course called, "Kingdom Identity." You can find it on www.chrisestrada.tv).

100

Ananias was oblivious that this man would write the Book of Romans. Let's face it, without the Book of Romans, we would all be a mess! In other words, he had no idea who he was ministering to. The same is true for us. We may be led to someone, but we have no idea they will be the next pop icon or the next world leader, and we would have no idea that this one encounter would be the door hinge that their entire life's focus and effort would hang on.

I pray God would raise and release Ananias's all over the world daily. Those who understand the Kingdom of God is not a matter of talk, but a matter of power (1 Corinthians 4:20). Men and women who will be filled with compassion and led by the Spirit to bring an encounter to those in their city.

HOW HE SPEAKS

The Ruined take up this call on their life and familiarize their hearts with His voice because they are trained to hear His whisper. The key to this is not just understanding that He wants to speak to you, but knowing how He speaks that makes the difference. Let me share a story to illustrate this.

I had a young man in my youth ministry who started to have these holy cravings to be used by God. He was always leading one of our treasure hunt teams and would always show up at church with a fresh testimony or a person he had just seen healed after he prayed for them and led them to Jesus.

There was nothing "Christian special" about this kid; he didn't even feel a call to ministry and had a different career goal. All he wanted was to be faithful and used of God. Erica and I were fine with this because we know The Ruined life is not just meant for the Church—but more so everywhere else.

One day, he was standing in line at the local grocery store to buy some things, and the Spirit of God moved on his heart. He didn't hear a voice or see a vision, but felt a nudge of the Holy Spirit to go and stand in the Pharmacy section. He was to pray for everyone who came to get their prescriptions. His heart filled with a promise—as many as he prayed for, that many would be healed.

He finished buying his items and quickly made his way to the Pharmacy. A woman had just finished paying for her prescription when he walked up. He told her his name, what church he was from, and he was there to pray for people who needed healing and breakthrough. The woman looked at him, shocked that a teenager would talk like this, but she said, "Sure, at this point, I'll do anything to get the pain out of my back."

Compassion filled his hearted, and he prayed simply, but with authority. He then asked the women to test her back and do something she couldn't do. She bent over and came back up with no pain. She bent over several more times just to make sure, but the same result. The pain was gone. She began to cry. She had the biggest smile on her face. She said, "Well, I guess I won't be needing these." She handed him her meds and walked off.

Just then an older gentleman, who had just finishing paying for his prescriptions, saw the woman get totally healed. So he said, "Would you do me, too?" The young man smiled and said, "Love too!" He prayed simply, but with authority and compassion for Jesus to heal his body. (He never asked what this man needed healing from). When he was done, he began to test out his hands, and said, "It worked! I have no more pain in my hands!" The man stood amazed, and my student smiled and began to preach salvation to him.

Then another man, who had just seen what had happened said, "Hey, I've been having all kinds of trouble in my body. Do you think Jesus could fix me up to?" He didn't even hesitate; he laid hands on this man, again praying short and simple, but with compassion and authority, flooding his heart. He saw another miracle. Before he knew it, he had a line forming for people to receive prayer from him.

He showed up to church later that night, holding a zip-lock bag full of pills. (At first, the youth pastor inside of me assumed he was trying to sell them to the other kids. That should give you an indication of what our Youth Ministry was made up of.) However, he told me everything that happened. He said, "Everyone I laid hands on got touched by God, and many handed me their prescription because they didn't need them anymore!"

We had a powerful service that night as we shared that testimony from the platform. I celebrate this young man's willingness to be used of God, live The Ruined Life, and go where God said to go!

We have to move past the fear of failure, rejection, and humiliation in this area of The Ruined Life. We cannot afford to live our lives held back by a score card we keep for every one of these areas. We incorrectly assume Jesus had to "spot check" every encounter with the Father, before He did anything: "Father, do you want me to heal this person? Do you want me to prophesy to this person? Do you want me to help this person?" Jesus lived, knowing it was the Fathers will and nature to heal, to speak to His people, and to serve mankind.

I'm often asked, "How do I know it's Jesus whose telling me to go and pray for that person's healing or to prophesy over another?" My answer is always really simple, "Well, the Devil would never tell you to heal someone; he would never show you how to partner with the Holy Spirit for someone's breakthrough, and he would never stir up a compassion for someone in need to encourage them. So there's only one other place directions like this could have come from."

I only answer it this way because I asked the Lord the same question, and this was His answer to me. I have never had the devil assist me on a treasure hunt and say, "Hey, Chris, you need to go and help that man over in the checkered shirt. I've been messing with him way too much, and he needs it."

The goodness of the Lord is many times what I'm led by, and I don't always need a Word of Knowledge to clue me in. If I see someone in a wheel chair, on crutches, or in a brace it stands out to me; I know God is leading me to pray for them.

COMPASSION

Whole books have been written about this subject, about how compassion works. I will give a simple perspective of compassion but I highly encourage you to study compassion thoroughly. It truly is life changing. To better understand compassion, let me tell you what it is not. Compassion is not sympathy; there's a big difference. Sympathy says, "I feel sorry for you," and that's it. Compassion says, "I feel sorry for you, and I'm inclined to do something about it." One leaves you like it met you, and the other, completely transforms you.

Jesus only operated out of compassion (Matthew 20:32-34, Mark 1:40-42, Mark 6:34, 8:2, Matthew 4:14, Matthew 9:35-38). You can fast, spend hours in a prayer room, or go to a powerful conference on "How To Heal The Sick," but if you lack compassion, you will lack authority. Compassion speaks because many times it is the voice of God.

TOP 3

God has more ways of speaking to us than we have of receiving His message. We all have a dominant way we hear Him, but we must never limit Him to speaking and leading us one way. I want to share the top three ways He does speak to us. The first is those who "hear his voice." You'll find He'll speaking in full sentences or as little as one word, but you hear Him more than anything.

The second is there are those of us who "see." You're quick to notice He'll cause floating thoughts, pictures or scenarios to play out in your mind, dreams, visions, symbols and signs, but you primarily "see" His leading.

Then there are those who "feel." (Personally, this is my dominant one). Many times, I feel impressed to act upon a gesture or a nudge in my heart. Those of us who "feel" sense a direction more than anything else as they are praying and ministering to people.

These are the top three ways I have discovered as I have trained thousands all over the world to do treasure hunts, and I'm constantly having to remind myself and others that we are not limited to just one way of receiving, as the Lord is not limited to one way of speaking. It's really never a question of, "Is He speaking?" It is the ability to distinguish the difference between His voice from the sound of others in our heart and head. The more time you feed on Him and hearing His voice, the easier He will be to identify.

TAKING RISKS

Risk taking is a part of the job description when it comes to The Ruined Life. It needs to be a habit we develop until it becomes a lifestyle and a normal part of our day. Erica and I travel all over the world, helping churches and ministries launch this kind of evangelistic ministry in their regions.

I remember when we were in Louisiana one year. We had just gotten done teaching out of Acts, chapter 9—literally the chapter you reading right now, and dismissed for lunch. The plan was for everyone to return after lunch, so we could organize teams and send them out for a few hours to serve and minister to people.

A sweet, older couple in the church was incredibly impacted by what they had just learned and felt provoked to skip lunch and go on a treasure hunt right then. They got in their pick-up truck and asked Holy Spirit for clues/words of knowledge, and He responded. He gave them an address to go to, and once they arrived, they were to ask for a man named

John, who was addicted to smoking weed, because Jesus wanted to deliver him.

They put the address in there GPS and found the home. When they knocked on the door it cracked open with a man who asked them what they wanted. So the older gentleman spoke up and told him why they were there. He said, "Hi, my name is Roy, and this is my wife, Jessica. We're from Life Church, and we're out praying for people today. God told us to come here and ask for a man named John who wants to be free from a drug addiction. Is there someone here who fits that description?"

The man threw open the door, took a long hit off of the joint he'd hidden behind his back, and while exhaling said, "Man, that's me, man. I can't get this stuff out of my life. Every time I try, (takes another hit off his joint), I always give into the urges I have. I hate this stuff, man!

Roy gently placed his hand on his shoulder, while Jessica placed her hand on the other shoulder. Roy said, "Now son, Jesus died for your sins, and that means he died for your freedom as well. We're going to pray, and you're going to be free from this forever." John began to weep at the sweet truth that was just spoken. Roy simply, but powerfully prayed, "Father, you led us to your son, John, and I declare him free from this drug addiction right now."

Then Jessica prayed for John and said, "Now baby, He loves you, and it's time to receive your freedom and His love for you." As soon as she was done speaking, the power of God hit John; he dropped right there at his front door. Laying on the ground with tears coming down his face and repentance coming out of his heart, he was having an encounter with Jesus. Roy and Jessica didn't know what to do as the Lord was ministering to John so they sat down on his front porch and waited.

A few minutes later, John sat up. He had the biggest smile on his face. Roy and Jessica prayed with him as he surrendered his life to Jesus and put his faith in Him. John's countenance was completely different as life, hope, and peace just entered into his heart. The couple exchanged information and encouraged John to come to church the next day. As they turned to walk away, John shouted at them and said, "Wait! Don't leave yet!" He ran back inside and was running all over the house gathering items into a little box. When he was done, he gave the box to the couple. They opened it and found that John had been gathering all of his sacks of weed, papers, pipes, and paraphernalia. He'd put it inside of this box for them to take away from him.

I remember coming back from lunch about to start mobilizing teams when this couple walked up to me, handed me the box, and told me what happened. I was shocked and excited! It wasn't a pastor or an evangelist who handed me this box. It was a couple who believed God would lead them, give them what they needed to say, and supply the power to minister to John.

I share this story and others because I don't want anyone to believe that these kind of encounters are reserved for spiritual giants. The Ruined are not 'one-man-show' with an itinerary and a book deal. The days of one-man armies are over, and the current movement on the Earth is being led by the believer.

Allow me to share another story with you. I had a student named Tracy, who got the oddest set of clues for an encounter. After a 15-minute session of leaning in and praying, she heard the Lord say, "Go to the gas station on the corner and meet a blind women named Ruth, who will be driving a car. I want you to lay hands on her and she is going to receive her sight." Tracy was instantly confused about why a blind woman would be driving? She brought it to me, asking what I thought. I asked her if she was absolutely sure she heard the Lord. She confirmed yes. So I prayed once more and off she went.

She scanned every car that came in to refuel, thinking any one of them could be this woman. She waited for two hours. Then a car jumped over the curb and caught her attention. She watched it barely miss hitting the gas pump, and then, park. A woman got out of the car disoriented. She started to put gas in her car. Tracy's heart knew this was Ruth. She approached her and said, "Hi, is your name Ruth?"

She responded, "Yes, baby."

"Mine name is Tracy, I go to Christ For The Nations, and we're out praying for people today. God told me to wait for you at this gas station because He wants to heal you. Do you have trouble seeing?"

Ruth broke out into a praise dance and said, "Now that's my Jesus lookin' out for me! C'mon girl, let's get to praying!"

After getting permission to lay hands on her eyes, Tracy very simply, but with authority, commanded her eye-sight to be restored in the name of Jesus. Ruth opened her eyes and could see with fully restored vision. She continued the praise service she started, except this time, Tracy joined in—full of wonder and excitement at what God had just done.

Tracy asked her how she could be driving if her eyesight was so bad. She said she was actually on her way to have corrective surgery, as she was legally blind. She couldn't find anyone to take her, so she, desperate for better eye sight, decided to drive herself and made an unplanned stop at this gas station on her way there.

I remember when Tracy returned back to share the testimony. It caused the whole class to be stirred for more! I've been asked many times if I get nervous when I go on treasure hunts or I approach someone who I feel God put on my heart to minister to. The answer is always, "Yes!"

The next question is usually, "How do you combat that nervousness?" My answer has always been the same. We have to know what our motivation is. My goal, when taking risks, is never to have something added to a spiritual highlight reel for Jesus and me to watch when I get to Heaven. It's to love, serve and impact people so they will surrender their lives to Him.

The truth is my numbers and spiritual success ratio used to drive my motivation, until one day I heard an evangelist say, "The number that concerns me isn't how many I led to Him. It's how many I could have led, but I was so busy being distracted with excuse-making and being nervous." My heart has never forgotten this! When this becomes our motivation, fueled by a desire to have an intimate relationship with Jesus, risk taking doesn't become uncomfortable—it's sin, sickness, and the devil that does!

BOLDNESS

Risk taking is natural to The Ruined, and it becomes our normal when we pursue this lifestyle. So many need an encounter with God, and it is up to us to bring them into that transforming moment. It's not enough to wear the uniform and have the right buzz words to make it seem like we are living The Ruined Life. There must be fruit and a trail of lives healed, changed, and restored everywhere we go. Many times, when I challenge people on this, I always hear the cry for more boldness. Early on, I prayed as if this was something God could just give me, but that's just not true.

Maybe you have cried out for the same thing. I want to encourage you with something that was later on said about Peter—after he was ruined, released healing on a beggar, and examined by the religious community. In Acts, chapter 4, the spiritual elite gathered to question if Peter and John had actually produced this miracle by using the authority in Jesus' name. What they observed perplexed them. The Bible says,

> *"When they saw the **boldness** of Peter and John, and perceived they were **uneducated and untrained** men, they marveled and realized **they had been with Jesus**"* (Acts 4:13, 14).

Notice the fruit of spending time with the Lord— Boldness starts to come out of your life. I remember one day, I was crying out for boldness, but felt I wasn't progressing. I said, "Lord, fill me with boldness. I want to win souls and impact lives."

The Lord gently responded, "Son, I don't give boldness, I develop it. You must allow me to condition your heart to take risks when I lead you to. If you keep ignoring it and making excuses for why you're not ready, you'll never develop boldness. You will become numb to my promptings and spiritually frustrated."

From that point forward, I began yielding when I felt God leading me to take a risk as I pursued The Ruined Life. There are some things God can't give, but He can develop them on the inside of you. Boldness, patience, authority, discernment, and more are all on the list of strengths God builds in us. Boldness makes the weak look strong, because when you are bold, you are under the influence of God's love and power, and you will go wherever He sends you and to whomever He sends you to. It's no longer about if we feel ready, or if we're strong enough. Godly boldness makes you completely dependent on Him and reprograms your heart and mind to respond when He leads you to. Taking risks will increase your level of boldness and authority, but you must be diligent to answer when He calls on you to an encounter.

REVIVAL CAN HAPPEN ANYWHERE, ANYTIME, WITH ANYONE

The Ruined live by this anthem, "Revival can happen anywhere, anytime, with anyone." I find it compelling that most of the ministry and miracles of Jesus happened outside of the synagogue and in the streets of Israel. Jesus' life has an emphasis on salvations, miracles, and deliverances happening anywhere.

From people's homes to their fishing businesses to even in places the spiritual culture of the day said was forbidden, Jesus brought life, power and hope everywhere he was being led to go. He even went to extremes measures to demonstrate it. He crossed a sea for one man's deliverance (Mark 4:35-5:1) and even interrupted funerals (Luke 7:11-15) because this is how the Kingdom of God works—without limits and a guaranteed, endless supply of anointing and authority.

The same should be true for the believer. We are not told to keep the supernatural power of God private when 90 percent of Jesus' miracles were public. We are really good about demonstrating the power of God in our churches, but it makes no sense for revival to hit our church, when the lost and hurting across the street have no idea what is taking place. This why the power of God has become so rare—we treat it likes its special when it should be normal.

The power of Almighty God was never meant to be secret, and when we keep it that way, we condition our people to only expect God to move in church and not shopping malls, gas stations, and restaurants. I've often challenged our students and staff to prophesy and release healing while they are shopping and going through the routine of their day. If we can't prophesy in grocery stores, like we do in altar calls, it's no wonder the world thinks the Church is so fake.

It's time for the real power of God to be carried by real lovers of Jesus to be released on real pain and needs in people's lives. My heart's cry is for a whole generation to be so ruined that they can't tell if they're at a church service or shopping at their favorite store, because people are laid out everywhere repenting, receiving, and responding to the revival move of God that just hit the place.

One day, I was leading a team on a treasure hunt, and we all wrote down the same store, so it was obviously clear that God wanted us to go there. We made our way there, full of expectation and ready to cause a 'Kingdom ruckus.' This was a massive store, but it seemed like we were the only ones in there. We had our clues, but when we saw someone, they didn't match anyone. Kind of frustrating when you're consumed with a godly passion to see lives transformed, but can't find who your are suppose to minister to.

So we regrouped in the back. We started praying for direction and for God to highlight someone. Just moments later, I saw a woman walking through the aisles. So knowing revival can happen anywhere, anytime, with anyone, I figured she had to be the one, since she was the only other one in the store besides us. She must be who we're here for. As I approached her, I started getting clues/words of knowledge about what was going on in her life. I said, "Ma'am, excuse me, but I'm from Christ For The Nations, and we're out praying for people today. Is your father in the hospital?"

Stunned she said, "Yes, how'd you know that?"

I said, "Ma'am, the Lord told me He is with your father, but he wants to minister to you."

Just then I started to see she was having night terrors and couldn't sleep because of her father. I sensed she had become so burdened in worry that she was concerned the health problems her father was having was about to start in her body and claim her life. I relayed these to her, and she began to weep, loudly in the store. Boldness filled my heart, and I began to cancel the attack of the enemy off of her life.

All of a sudden, she turned stiff and glared at me, dead in my eye. I could tell she was trying to speak, but just couldn't. I knew then she was manifesting a demon. It was time for freedom to come into this women's life. I rebuked the demons claim and commanded it to leave. I declared, "Ma'am, you're free from this because of what Jesus has done for you on the cross."

The power of God hit this woman, and she went out right in the aisle. I turned around and noticed we were now surrounded by people—all wondering what was happening. Immediately, one of my students spoke up and said, "The love and power of Jesus is freeing this woman right now. If you have any sickness or addictions in your life, come over here so we can pray for you. Jesus is going to heal you." Every person came forward. I watched, proudly amazed as our team began to minister to every person.

I continued ministering freedom to this woman until she came out of it and stood up. She gave her life to Jesus right then. We ministered in that store for over an hour that day with people getting healed from all types of pains, past hurts, and free from addictions. Most everyone gave their life to Jesus, as well. Why would this happen? Because a group of devoted ones believed revival could happen anywhere, anytime, with anyone! It's time for store aisles to become altars and for every place we shop to become dangerous ground for sin and sickness.

We've had people driving down the road, asked to be pulled over because some of our people noticed they had hearing aids, shoulder slings, and wheel chairs in the backseat. More often than not, these people receive a miracle. Why? Because revival can happen anywhere, anytime, with anyone!

My wife used to work as a receptionist at a friend of ours Doctor's office once a week. One morning, the Lord showed her a certain woman. He gave Erica her name and what she needed prayer for. Erica, being a pro at this, wrote down the clues and went into work that morning. Just after lunch, the exact women she saw in the morning, walked through the door. Erica knew this was a Divine opportunity, but wanted to look for the right time to minister to this woman.

As she came out from seeing the Doctor, she was visibly upset with tears coming down her face. When the women was going to pay for the appointment, she came up to Erica's window. Without looking at any of the paper work, Erica asked if her name was Lucy. She nodded yes. Erica said, "Lucy, I'm a Christian, and God speaks to me. He showed me you would be coming in today, and that you would be diagnosed with Cancer. I don't want to be too pushy, but if that's true, I believe he wants to heal you right now."

Lucy stood there stunned! Erica asked her if she could pray with her. Erica came around to the reception area and held Lucy's hand as she declared healing over her body. Erica began to prophesy over this women and she was receiving the encouragement and comfort the Lord was supplying. When she was done, Lucy confirmed everything that was said to her and walked away powerfully touched. (We don't know if she was fully healed from Cancer, but one thing is for sure, she left the Doctor's office full of life and hope.) Again, how could this happen? Because revival can happen anywhere, anytime with anyone!

None of these testimonies happened at a conference or a church service. They happened where miracles don't normally happen. I declare to you The Ruined are being mobilized all over the Earth, and what used to be uncommon places for the power of God to move, will become common, because revival can happen anywhere, anytime, with anyone!

HEART & GOALS OF A TREASURE HUNT

The Ruined have two simple goals as they treasure hunt. All of these goals are done with a heart of a servant. We've all been around opinionated and obnoxious Christians, who try to push their agendas on people. This is not the attitude or the heart behind a treasure hunt. I have been rejected or just flat out yelled at and told, "No, I don't want to be prayed for!" When this happens, I yield and go about my day because I don't want to build up a wall and harden someone's heart because I wanted to impose my spiritual will on them simply because I have a "word" for them.

I am on this planet as a servant and a steward—nothing more. I live to serve Jesus and the people He loves. If I don't carry this kind of attitude and approach people like this, I will be met with resistance. A servant-oriented heart and mind disarms a lot of people, so they can receive the blessing and freedom Jesus wants them to have. We must release revival as servants. On our staff we have a motto, "We serve like kings and we rule like servants!" (Thank you, Bill Johnson, for sharing this great truth!) We are a "royal priest hood and a holy nation" (1 Peter 2:9), and we should live our lives exactly like this.

The two goals of a Treasure Hunt are:
1.   Demonstrate The Love and Power of Jesus
2.   Present The gospel message of Jesus

This is illustrated perfectly in Jeff's story. Jeff is a leader in our church and was pursuing The Ruined Life. One day, as he was driving home, he heard the Lord begin to drop clues in his heart. Jeff was to go to this particular grocery store, go to where the cereal is sold, and he would meet a man covered in tattoos. Jeff was to pray for this man's back to be healed, which will serve as a sign to this man and he would surrender his life to Jesus.

Jeff quickly drove to the grocery store and went to the cereal aisle, but he didn't see anyone. Convinced he was led by God, he walked around the store, waiting for this man to show up. The third time he checked the cereal aisle, he saw a tall, muscular man, who was covered in tattoos. He was dressed in black leather pants, with a black leather vest, with no shirt under it. His chest was bare, and he wore black boots.

Jeff was instantly taken back, but remembered the motto of The Ruined Life: Revival can happen anywhere, anytime, with anyone. Very politely, Jeff approached the man, who was holding a box of cereal and said, "Sir, my name is Jeff. I'm a Christian, and God speaks to me. Jesus asked if I would come pray for a man with a lot of tattoos because he has a hurt back, but He wants to heal it. I think you're that man. May I pray for you?"

The man sharply questioned, "Who told you that!?" Jeff said, "Sir, Jesus did. Would you be okay if I prayed for you?" The mountain of a man replied, "Yeah, sure." Jeff prayed simply, but with authority. He prayed, "Jesus you sent me here because you love this man. I believe you want to heal his back, so I command it to be healed and all the pain to leave now."

Just then the man jumped up a little and said, "Whoa! What was that?"

Jeff, sensing the power of God hitting this guys back, said, "Sir, Jesus just healed your back. Try and do something you couldn't do before we prayed."

The man bent over, stayed like that for a moment and came back up with an astonished look on his face. He couldn't believe he wasn't in pain, so he bent over again. When he came back up, tears started to form in his eyes. He was still shocked by what was happening. He bent over again, just to make sure he was really pain free a third time. When he came back up, He said, "Who told you I had a hurt back?"

Jeff, being full of boldness, said, "Sir, it was Jesus and He loves you so much that He died and rose from the dead so you could have this healing and eternal life. Have you ever made Jesus your Lord and Savior?"

This man shook his head no. Jeff asked if he wanted to, and with a grin, he said, "Yes!" Jeff led the man to Jesus right then. Powerful!

We must remember that what is going to populate Heaven is not our ministries, miracles, and prophetic words. It's people! The most biblical way to get as many people there is to preach His gospel and demonstrate His love and power. Of course, there are more ways to demonstrate Him than healing and prophesying to people. I have paid for meals and coffees just to demonstrate a form of Jesus' love through generosity, which has led me to be able to witness to them. Sometimes, all that was needed to demonstrate was a little bit of care and good manners, which led to a moment to witness to people.

The Ruined are not dogmatic about there being only a few ways to win souls. We just need to make sure we carry the heart of a servant when we demonstrate and share the message of Jesus.

TREASURE HUNT MAP

I'm sure by now you've picked up a pattern and a little bit of the language it takes to go on a Treasure Hunt, but let's fill in any gaps, so we can increase your effectiveness and productivity. (2 Peter 1:3-8).

First, we pray! Not profound, but true, except I always keep this time short. Most people feel the need to pray for hours when their doing anything, but the truth is in the real world you don't get any preparation time. Clues can drop on you and ministry could be needed in a moment, so we need to condition ourselves to be ready. To accomplish this, I usually only give 10, at the most 15 minutes to pray, receive from the Lord, and write down the clues that were given. This also helps when there isn't an organized treasure hunt. You could be shopping or having dinner somewhere and God begins to speak to you about someone. When you live like this long enough you become sensitive to a sense of urgency and will 99 percent of the time need to respond quickly to the Lord's direction.

We've ministered to people who were being bombarded with suicidal thoughts. A Ruined one happened to be walking past them when the Lord quickened them to minister life and freedom. He can call on us quickly, and we don't always get to or need to know what we will say. It's just important that we respond and remain faithful.

The second, but also goes along with the first, is filling in the treasure hunt map. Usually, toward the end, I ask people to begin writing what they were hearing, seeing, or sensing as they were praying. It used to amaze me how many times my mind would go blank at this very moment. I found the only reason this happens is because I was qualifying every thought and tried to make sure each clue/word of knowledge was spiritual, powerful, and holy enough to guide me. I was totally unaware at the time of how creative and specific God could be.

I've seen clues like crying, birthday cake, broken home, and a bus stop. When one of our teams saw a woman holding a birthday cake and a red balloon, while crying at a bus stop they passed every day, they asked why. They found out this Mom had a report filed against her of child neglect. Her children were removed by social services, and she was on her way to a supervised visit for her daughter's birthday.

Part of the team prayed and comforted her, while another part went into the store to buy more presents for the little girl's birthday. The mothers face lit up with gratefulness and joy as her bus came. She texted us a few weeks later that she got her baby girl back in weeks, and not months, and she had started to attend a life-giving church.

The clues of crying, birthday cake, broken home, and a bus stop could have easily been dismissed as random, but God knows every detail of everyone's life, and He loves to show it.

I encourage you to treat every thought as if it was whispered from Jesus. Even if you don't use every clue, just be grateful that one of them could bring someone closer to Him.

I've included a copy of the treasure hunt map below to show you what ours looks like. We use the Treasure Hunt Map Kevin Dedmon shares in his book, *The Ultimate Treasure Hunt*. I encourage you to read it, as it is extensive in what a treasure hunt should look like.

The Treasure Map

Each person writes down Words of Knowledge in the spaces allowed for each category

- **Location** (stop sign, bench, digital clock, coffee shop, Target, Wal-Mart, etc.)

  _____ _____ _____ _____
  _____ _____ _____

- **A person's name**

  _____ _____ _____ _____
  _____ _____ _____

- **A person's appearance** (the color of their specific articles of clothing, the color of their hair, etc.)

  _____ _____ _____ _____
  _____ _____ _____

- **What they might need prayer for** (knee brace, cane, kidneys, tumor, left ankle, marriage, etc.)

  _____ _____ _____ _____
  _____ _____ _____

- **The unusual** (lollipop, windmill, lime-green door, dolphins, etc.)

_____ _____ _____ _____

_____ _____ _____

Once you find your Treasure:

1) Walk up to them and say, "Hi, My name is _____ and I'm from (Church/Ministry). We're out praying for people today, and I think I'm supposed to pray for you." Then explain the treasure hunt to them by showing your Treasure Map.
2) If they'd like prayer, ask them to briefly tell you what they need prayer for and if you can lay hands on them to pray for them. (Only two people need to approach someone when on a treasure hunt and always take a member of the opposite sex with you when praying for them.)
3) Invite God's presence. Ask His Kingdom to come. Pray simple, but with authority.
4) Listen for promptings of the Holy Spirit to pray in certain ways or to follow certain strategies. Remain willing to take risks.
5) Keep your eyes open while you pray, watch for visible signs of God's action in or on the person
6) Ask the person, "Are you feeling anything?"
7) Ask the person to test it out, to move or do something that was impossible or too painful before they received

their healing. Another way of asking, "Try to cause the pain you experienced before. See if it's gone."

8) If the person is healed, rejoice together and give praise to God. Encourage the person to obtain a doctor's report for a physical healing, especially for their safety.

9) Ask them if they have ever accepted Jesus into their life. If no, share your testimony and offer to pray with them. Then invite them to your church!

Usually, before we prayed, we placed everyone into groups. So it's at this time I ask the groups to share their clues with each other, select a driver and make a decision on where they will head off to first. I pray one last prayer for increased awareness of God's presence, for them to be filled with power, and then we all go out.

TESTIMONIES

Testimonies are a huge part of a treasure hunt and The Ruined Life. One of the three ways we overcome the enemy is by our testimony. (Revelations 12:11). The Ruined will find that testimonies stir their heart to hunger for more of Him and to be used by Him when they hear testimonies.

I have found the quickest way to become discouraged is to focus on what God hasn't done, instead of what He is doing. However, when I focus on what He has done (Testimonies), what He is doing (Victorious living), and what He is going to do (His promises), it's a shield of courage that nothing can penetrate. Testimonies create that for us.

Psalm 37:3 says to, "Feed on His faithfulness." We have

to draw strength from what we have seen Him do and the best way is to celebrate that. This is why you should always carve about 30 minutes or more for people to share fresh testimonies as soon as they get back from treasure hunting. It will stir every heart in the room!

TIPS

Here's a few more tips to help you as you Treasure Hunt:

- Always pray with your eyes open—This is for everyone's safety and to be sensitive to what's happening.

- Maybe you're in the middle of a Treasure Hunt and you're saying, "What if I don't find anyone?" Stop, find a place to pray, ask God to highlight someone to you and go for it! It doesn't matter if they match what clues you have, just go for it. The map is not doing the guiding, He is.

- As you are praying for someone, be listening. Many times, the Lord will add to what you're praying, and you may end up prophesying or getting more words of knowledge

- Do not pray for employees or people working. We want to honor all places of business, and these people are there to work. Having said that, I usually throw out a list of ridiculous and almost impossible signs for people to look for when they fill drawn to minister to an employee. Normally, it sounds something like this: "Please don't pray for employees, unless you see an elephant with seven squirrels riding on their back, and you hear seven trumpet blasts, and then a Ninja will hold up a flag that says, "Encounter," while an angel is walking you over to them."

Believe it or not, I have had on two occasions, where all of my crazy criteria was met, and there was a strong move of God on those two people. But, I always preference keeping ministry to employees off limits.

YOU'RE READY

After reading this I am sure you're brewing with faith for people to encounter God. I want to tell you, you're ready! God is watching over your life, looking for the opportunity to "make your efforts successful" (Psalm 37:3). I would like to take the opportunity to pray over you like I do our teams when we are being sent out.

"Father, I declare clarity to hear Your voice over Your sons and daughters. As they are sent out, I pray for an increase in their awareness of Your Presence. I declare these signs will follow those who believe, 'In My name they will cast out demons; they will speak with new tongues; they will take up serpents; and if they drink anything deadly, it will by no means hurt them; they will lay hands on the sick, and they will recover' (Mark 16:17, 18). We desire to honor you and have 'Your kingdom come, Your will be done, on earth as it is in heaven' (Mark 6:9-10). Today, I declare they are willing to play whatever role you need them to play so that one more soul can come to Christ. If

our duty is to plant, we will plant. If it's our duty to water, we will water. If it's our duty to reap, we will reap. We focus our motives to be faithful and serve You and people with the right attitude. I declare they will be full of developed courage and boldness to present and demonstrate your love and power. God, You are with those who go, so I ask that these will go swiftly and powerfully into every region and release the power of Jesus. In your precious name we ask this.
Amen!"

WHAT YOU REALLY NEED

The ruined are not like most people who need all the boxes checked and lists cross checked. They are allowed a seasons of training, but they are encouraged not to become addicted to the training. What they need most is not more equipping, but they need more courage. In the next chapter, you will learn what courage is and what it isn't, and how we develop it, so we can have a sustained life of love, courage, and power! Get ready, the next chapter should come with a warning label. It will ruin you!

Chapter 6

RELEASING REVIVALISTS

Growing up, I had a dream of someday playing in the NBA. I would look for a place to play all the time. It didn't matter if it was a park, open gym at school, or a pick-up game at the local college. I knew I would need to devote a huge amount of time to practice, and I was looking to play in places with players that were better than I was, so I could stay ahead of my competition. It was my life's goal and passion.

I remember one day, I came home to find my dad had bought a basketball hoop. I was thrilled because it meant I didn't have to go to gyms all day. I could play at home for longer periods of time. One day, I had been shooting around all day when one of my older brothers came out and said, "Chris, why do you practice all the time?"

Now, I knew what he was there to do. If you have older brothers, you understand they are dangerous, and they love nothing more than to pick on you. So I fired back, "Cause I might buy you a house someday?" I wasn't gonna let him get to me.

He smirked and said, "Yeah, okay. No, seriously, why do you try so hard?"

I was determined to not let him phase me, so I said, "I might buy you a car, too, if you shut up!"

I was trying hard to stand my ground and not let him get

to me. But what he said next, I wasn't ready for. I never realized how much my confidence would be shaken or how insecure I would become. After hearing his last comment, I went from being able to hit from anywhere on the court, to not even being able to make a layup.

He said, "Come on Chris! Get real! Do you really think you're good enough to make it into the NBA?"

I never had anyone question my dream like that before. For the first time, I found out my plan was not possible—I could fail.

I remember a similar moment with my son, Elisha. I was walking him to his preschool. He suddenly stopped, tugged on my arm, and looking at me with his chocolate brown eyes said, "Dad, when I grow up, I want to be just like you." But what he finished the sentence with, I wasn't ready for. He was looking at me as if he was staring into my soul. He said, "Dad, when I grow up, I want to be just like you or a dinosaur!"

I laughed so hard, but judging by the look on his face, he was dead serious. What kind of father would I be if my son had said he wanted to be a doctor, or own his own business, or play in the NBA, and I responded, "Come on, Elisha. Get real! Do you really think your good enough to do any of those things?" The amount of discouragement that hits us, when our dream, calling or assignment is reality checked, can undo us so fast! We must learn how to guard our courage.

We must be careful to be enticed when we hear the words, "Get real." I'm convinced too many times we buy into too much of this thing called "reality." God doesn't live in reality. He is not bound by time, preference, and circumstance. God is not intimidated by stats, facts, and history. Odds do not apply to God, so they do not apply to the sons and daughters of God. We don't allow ourselves to take risks and release revival anymore, because we've over eaten on reality. I can always tell when I've had too much "reality." I have this addiction to wanting to "feel ready." Which will never happen. God never said you'd be ready. He said,

> "... *Eye has not seen, nor ear heard, Nor have entered into the heart of man The things which God has prepared for those who love Him"* (1 Corinthians 2:9).

The Bible is not full of people who had a plan. Sometimes, we should circle back and see who He chose to use to expand His Kingdom. Here's a small recap: Abraham was too old; yet, he became a father when it was physically impossible. Gideon was too scared; yet, he defeated a massive army with 300 men, and they had no weapons! Mary, the mother of Jesus, was still a virgin, but got pregnant! He never said we would be ready. He said He would be with us (Deuteronomy 31:8, Isaiah 43:10, Matthew 28:10), never leave us, and in the moment, He will give us what to say (Matthew 10:19, Mark 13:11, Luke 12:11).

The Ruined must remember we are called to live an unpredictable lifestyle. The biggest reason why people subscribe to reality and struggle with their calling is because of one word: Discouragement. Here's a picture definition of discouragement. It means to take courage out of someone's

131

heart. The opposite of discouragement is encouragement, which means to take courage and put it in someone's heart.

Friend, are you settling because you stepped out in faith to go after your destiny, only to trip, stall, or fail? We settle too easily in our marriages, in our businesses, or in the promises of God over our lives because we've allowed discouragement to remain far too long. My wife and I have a huge heart to encourage people as it's a part of our ministry's vision—"To release courage and power to risk takers and dreamers, who desire Divine-turnarounds."

This is a bed some of the Israelites could have been lying in, if they had let discouragement do the guiding and supplying, instead of courage.

In Judges, chapter 20, there are 12 tribes that made up the nation of Israel. Men from the tribe of Benjamin do a wicked thing to a man from the tribe of the Levites. This man from the tribe of the Levites demands a military response be brought against Benjamin. So the 11 other tribes gather 400,000 men. When the tribe of Benjamin hears that war is upon them, they gather 26,000 men. This is setup to be a quick battle! Read what happens next:

> *"The Israelites went up to Bethel and inquired*
> *of God. They said, 'Who of us is to go up first to*
> *fight against the Benjamites?'*
> *"The LORD replied, 'Judah shall go first.'*
> *"The next morning the Israelites got up and*
> *pitched camp near Gibeah. The Israelites went*
> *out to fight the Benjamites and took up battle*

positions against them at Gibeah. The Benjamites came out of Gibeah and cut down twenty-two thousand Israelites on the battlefield that day" (Judges 20:18-21).

Have you ever felt God tell you to do something? Have you ever had enough courage and boldness to go and do it, and then you fail!? This is exactly what happened with the Israelites. God not only tells them to go to battle, but He chooses their battle formation and positions the tribe of Judah to go first. I have learned a secret when it comes to risk taking. If I ever want to confuse my enemy (the devil, fear, discouragement, insecurity, etc.), I just need to throw the party a little bit early and praise my way before I take the risk. Praise Him, while I'm taking the risk. Praise Him after I take the risk, no matter what the outcome is.

This is the focus of The Ruined Life, as we desire to release revival everywhere we go. Lately, revival has become a buzzword, which is creating many perspectives on what it looks like. The definition I subscribe to is Revival is an unexpected move of God that brings dead things to life. Revival is not more meetings, conference, and gatherings. I'm for all of that because they give us community and keep us on the same page to have a unified vision. But I burn for sustained revival. The only way we can sustain revival is if it becomes our lifestyle! The Ruined are revivalists—people who are willing to be used by God to do whatever, whenever, however!

FIGHT DISCOURAGEMENT WITH ENCOURAGEMENT

We all can identify with the discouragement Israel is feeling after losing 22,000 men in a battle the Lord sends them into. Benjamin is outnumbered 15 to 1, and they cut down 22,000 men without losing a single man. This kind of "loss" is deflating. It's like laying hands on people for healing and they don't receive it; witnessing to someone you've been praying for only to be met with walls; Standing on God's Word without seeing your circumstances change. It's defeating, but The Ruined must still guard their hearts.

The best way we can protect our heart from the heaviness of discouragement is to counter it with radical courage. Defeat your discouragement by doing something that requires a massive amount of encouragement. This is why risk-taking must become a lifestyle. Taking risks doesn't just release the love and power of Jesus, but it feeds and strengthens our hearts! Some of the greatest testimonies I've ever heard have a common thread woven in them. They happened in the middle of people's greatest challenges and seasons.

Again, this is another piece of The Ruined Life. We become so ruined, we don't respond how we used to or the way others around us do, when it comes time to face discouragement and challenges. We ambush the enemy by our strong trust in God and display aggressive courage. Thinking about this reminds me of one of my favorite testimonies comes from one of our leaders.

I remember I was reading my Bible early on a Monday morning when my phone rang. Seeing it was one of our leaders named Jasmine, I answered, and she demanded she needed to talk to me. I told her, "We're on the phone talking—so let's talk." But she insisted we talk face to face. So with my wife's permission, I picked her up. We went to a fast food restaurant, and while sitting in the drive through for some breakfast, I turned to her and asked, "Jasmine, what was so important that you couldn't talk to me over the phone?" She held up her pointer finger on one hand, and with the other, she pushed back her hair. In an intense way she said, "Alright, Pastor Chris, you need to listen."

Having a wife and two daughters, I've learned something about the female race. When you raise your pointer finger on your hand, it gives your neck permission to be 30 feet longer than it was 1.7 seconds earlier. You can go from girl to giraffe faster than my jaw can drop from watching it happen. I'm pretty sure both sides of her head touched my car as she said, "Alright, Pastor Chris, you need to listen." So, knowing all that was happening, simultaneously with her saying, "Alright, Pastor Chris, you need to listen," you can imagine how intense it got in my car.

Jasmine continued to say, "On Friday, I was given an assignment in my speech class. I am supposed to give a two minute speech on something significant that happened in my life."

I responded, "Well, Jasmine, I'll pray you do a good job."

"Thank you, PC, but on Saturday, I was praying and Holy Spirit spoke to me. He said He wanted me to share my testimony as my speech because that's something significant in my life."

Like all Youth Pastors would, I yelled back, "Jasmine, you have to do that! You gotta do this! You betta not be a cissy and not follow through with this." Listen, when a Youth Pastor has one of their students tell them they're going to take a stand for Jesus, we get overly excited. My reaction surprised her, but she said, "PC, I'm going to do it, but I wanted to talk with you so you could coach me on how to share my testimony."

"Jasmine, I need you to focus." You can imagine how intense I got for the rest of this car ride. I reminded her the importance of sharing her testimony was to tell others of all the powerful things God has done for you. It really bothers me when 90 percent of people's testimonies focus on the garbage and junk that was going in their lives before they met Jesus. Then what Jesus did for them is only for the other 10 percent. God gets little glory for that. The world doesn't want to know what you were like when you were in the world. They want to know what you've been like since you left the world and gave your life to Jesus!

I shared this truth with Jasmine as we pulled up to her school. We had a few extra minutes to spare, so I turned up the worship music, stretched out her hands, and started praying for her, her class, the school, and every student who walked in front of my car on their way into school. When it was time to go I told Jasmine I wanted her to call me as soon as she could. She agreed and ran off to class.

Her speech class was her second period class. She sat through her entire first period class praying in the spirit. It's all she could do, anticipating what she was about to do next. Before she knew it, the bell rang and the moment was fast approaching.

Let me stop the story right here. All of us know what this moment feels like. Right before you're about to do what God has asked you to do, have you noticed all the butterflies that come up in your stomach? It's like all of your innards start to have intense fellowship, while you lose your appetite completely. You even start praying things that don't even make sense. Things like, "God, you ready? You sure you want to do this? I'm just checking on you because I don't want to force you into anything. You good? You sure?"

These are the moments discouragement likes to paralyze our Kingdom efforts on the Earth. It causes us to get so focused on everything that could go wrong or us making a fool of ourselves that we forget to draw from the reservoir of courage. When we give into this, we either don't follow through with our assignment, or we only partially go through with what He assigned to us. Discouragement robs us of so much. We must meet it head on, with blunt courage. Let's pick up the story now.

With all the thoughts of embarrassing herself swirling around in her and "ruining" her reputation, by the time she got to her class, she had convinced herself she wasn't going to go through with any of what she had in her heart. She sat in her chair, trying to make herself look invisible.

Her teacher started the class, reminding them of their assignment. She asked if there were any volunteers. One student volunteered, came to the front of the class, gave their speech, and then sat back down. The teacher asked again if there were any volunteers. No one volunteered, so the teacher scanned the room and finally said, "Jasmine, your next. Come on up and share your speech with us."

Jasmine's heart sank while her jaw dropped. I've had plenty of internal conversations like this. They go something like, "Oh, Lord, that's not right. I'm going to do it, but you play too much, and we need to talk about this later."

Jasmine approached the front, still in shock, but she knew the only thing she had prepared was to give her testimony. So, she just went for it. (God is with those who "go," even if He has to give us the loving "shove" of destiny! Ha!) Jasmine began, "Today, I want to share a significant moment in my life. It was the day I gave my life to Jesus."

In just one moment, it was like all the air had been sucked out of the room of this public high school. Even the teacher was now listening, intently, to every word Jasmine was saying. Jasmine continued, "A lot of you know me and how I used to get into trouble all the time. I used to fight a lot. I used to party a lot. I used to get high all the time." She then pointed at a kid in the class and said, "Remember, we used to get high all the time." This kid just sank in their chair, pretending not to know what she was talking about.

Jasmine kept going. "But then a friend of mine invited me to church, so I went. I liked it, so I went back the next week. I felt like the people were nice, so I went back a third week. I knew God was speaking to me, so I went back a fourth week."

Now, I remember when Jasmine came back that fourth week. We had just finished our pre-service prayer and opened the doors for students to flood our little store front church. The prayer time was powerful, and we could all sense God's presence lingering in the room. As students were rushing in, Jasmine put one foot inside of our sanctuary and fell on the ground under the power of God. She began screaming and surrendering her life to God. It shocked some and thrilled others, but being that our church was so tiny, we didn't have anywhere to carry her.

So we had a couple of leaders praying for her as we went on with service. She screamed, cried, laughed, and worshipped throughout the whole service. It was a powerful night. When she got up off the floor, she was a totally different person. She went home and told her brothers what happened, and the next week, they came to church and got saved. It was amazing and beautiful, as I had front row seats to it all happening.

When Jasmine was sharing this part in her "speech," she began to notice students who were starting to cry, while others were hanging on her every word. She sensed boldness fill her heart. Then, she saw a cheerleader in the front row who had a knee brace on. Knowing our value for "presentation and demonstration," she told the girl, "God just healed your knee. Take it out of the knee brace and walk on it." The girl didn't even hesitate. She took off her knee brace and noticed the pain and discomfort was gone—joy rushed into her heart.

Now, the whole class is embracing everything that is happening in the classroom. Jasmine then turned to a football player in the back who had his arm in a sling. She boldly said,

"Hey! God just healed your arm. Take your arm out of that sling, and do what you couldn't do before." God totally healed this guys' arm in front of the whole class.

Then Jasmine turned to the teacher (I know! Go big or go home!), and said, "Ma'am, you've doubted whether God is real since you were a little girl and these two miracles are signs to you that He is real." Jasmine threw out her arm in that direction, and the power of God hit the teacher, who fell onto the floor and had a two-minute visitation from Jesus. She had been brought up believing in a different religion. (I asked Jasmine later why she threw out her arm, and she said, "I don't know. I've watched you do that and thought there was something special to it." Ha! Truly, those we lead are watching every little thing we do!)

The teacher got up from the floor and ran out of the classroom. As Jasmine saw this she thought, "Well if I'm going to get arrested, I might as well make this look good." Jasmine continued in words of knowledge as she began to minister to other students about addictions, unplanned pregnancies and healing.

The teacher had actually run to the teachers' lounge, where she found other teachers taking a break. She said, "You have to come to my classroom. Stop what you're doing! Come here!" She brought the rest of the teachers in as Jasmine was ministering. She lined up all the other teachers against the wall, pointed to Jasmine, and said, "Okay, now do it again. Do what you just did to me, to them."

Jasmine laid hands on every teacher and began to tell them things that they had only shared with their spouse and close friends. Now, I know there maybe some skeptics who are thinking, "How do I know this really happened."

Well, I got a call from Jasmine and the assistant principal. Jasmine was crazy excited about what had just happened, and the assistant principal was really nervous because of the way Jasmine described what happened. The assistant principal asked me, "Pastor Estrada, we've had some unique events today. Sir, could you tell us what a "glory bomb" is?" Which is the phrase Jasmine used to describe what just happened in her speech class.

I cannot tell you how long I prayed for encounters like this, but soon enough this would become common in our church. We sought Jesus, boldness filled our heart, and when Heaven directed us, we responded. If discouragement showed up along the journey, that was only a signal to us to increase the risk and combat it with fearless courage.

RISK TAKERS

Why would something like that happen for Jasmine? Because she decided to take a risk and overcome discouragement with courage. The difference isn't God only uses "certain special people." The problem is only certain people let God use them. The Ruined understand the truth found in 1 Corinthians 4:20,

"For the kingdom of God is not in word but in power."

Jasmine knew it wasn't just her words, but her trust in God's power that would bring people into the Kingdom.

I love sharing this story because the demonstration of God's power didn't happen in a church or conference. It happened in a classroom. The Ruined are not thrown off by the setting their led to take a Kingdom risk in because they are people who are attracted to risk-taking.

The issue people will have with The Ruined is they are constantly in over their heads and they're always taking risks, but that's the trait of someone whose been ruined! The Ruined understand that Jesus didn't die so we can play it safe. He didn't give you the natural abilities and gifting you possess so you can live intimidated and scared the rest of your life. He died to give you authority, so no matter what the odds are, you will be successful.

As you are reading this, I want you to realize, you are not God's back up plan. You are His battle strategy. It's time to get comfortable with living in risk because you've been ruined from comfortable and casual. When you are ruined, you've sabotaged your desire for easy and possible and have started to feed yourself off of risk and fearlessness. It's time for the fearless ruined to influence regions and nations. Why?

Because you can't stop the fearless. You can't argue with the fearless. You can't intimidate the fearless. The fearless ruined refuse to change the subject. They are freedom fighters. They will waste their lives on a holy pursuit of releasing the love and power of Jesus, everywhere they go. The fearless ruined will not be known by their degrees and their titles. They will be known by their faith and their hunger. The next move of the Holy Spirit belongs to the fearless ruined!

REDRAW THE BATTLE LINES

Let's look back on Judges, chapter 20, to see how Israel battled through their discouragement. Even though they had a much larger army, they suffered a depressing loss. Yet, I love what they do next.

> *"But the Israelites encouraged one another and again took up their positions where they had stationed themselves the first day"* (Judges 20:22).

Instead of sulking and complaining, they "encouraged one another" and went back to the first place they drew their battle line. I believe many are reading this and wondering, "Where and when should I start living a Ruined Life?" I declare to you now is the time. Start out with allowing courage to flood your every thought and action. Then draw your battle line. When you see a person or situation that has crossed it, realize now you have godly authority to minister.

I want you to notice they didn't just encourage themselves. They also went back to where they had suffered loss. Don't give the enemy one inch. Say you step out to pray for someone's hearing; yet, nothing happens. You leave that encounter feeling like you "missed it." Then the next day you get the same opportunity to pray for someone to receive their healing. Don't hesitate—approach that encounter with the same confidence and assurance you had the day before. All you have to do is redraw the battle at the same place you drew it before. God is not looking at your success ratios. He wants to know you're reliable and haven't let the distraction of discouragement change your dependability.

In 2010, I was praying over several issues that were negatively impacting society today. I recognized I was praying from a depth I hadn't prayed before over these attacks. When I caught myself saying, "Lord, what is your response to the abortion issue? What is your response to the redefining of marriage? What is your strategy for the deception on the Earth right now?"

From one moment to the next, I had a vision. I saw an ocean of people ready, but waiting to be sent all over the Earth to transform it. I saw Jesus walking in between the rows of people, and He would stop at each one, taking a moment to write on them, and then move on to the next.

In the next moment, I was walking next to the Lord. When He stopped at each person, I was able to read what He was writing on each one of them. He was placing a "Hello, my name is" sticker on them, and then writing a word in the blank section of the sticker. It was in this moment I could hear my cries echoing in the vision.

"Lord, what is your response?"

"What is your strategy?"

Then I heard Him say, "I am changing the name of this generation. They have been labeled, lazy, apathetic, and entitled. I am giving them a Jacob moment, and their name will be Revival!"

My life and heart continues to draw from this vision, knowing that what He showed me then is what is taking place

144

all over the world. I have seen this promise being fulfilled from Brazil to Australia, to Europe and Asia. I cannot tell you how many cities and nations I've preached in where I've been directed to give out, "Hello, my name is" stickers with the name "Revival" written on it. I have had to replace many on the front of my Bible as it's a reminder of why and what I'm believing for. I've seen them on car windows, desks, and displayed on banners in churches. Holy Spirit is accelerating this call across the planet and The Ruined are responding.

BREAKING NEWS

I've got news for the world! It's time to begin the conversation with the world—The Ruined are rising! They're taking their place in the global Kingdom strategy of walking in holiness, truth, faith, and grace, while releasing unconditional love and supernatural power. The days are coming when we will hear of cancer treatment centers shutting down because The Ruined have erased cancer from their city, demonstrating the power of almighty God. The day will come when 20-year heroin addictions will be undone by the power of the Holy Spirit.

I can see people coming out of bars, strip clubs, and crack houses, sitting down to eat at a restaurant, when someone who has been ruined is in the same place and receives instructions to go and minister to them. The Ruined who are ensuring this generation will not have a spiritual drought, but a spiritual depth unlike any other. I see ruthless courage assaulting the kingdom of darkness, while advancing the Lordship of Jesus Christ. The

Ruined will carry Divine focus, holy expectation, and dangerous hope. The Ruined will not be casual, but deliberate with every moment entrusted to them. They will know every assignment will have an eternal impact. I declare you are a part of The Ruined. Every minute of your life will be filled with purpose and direction. Separate yourself to Him. Live fearlessly. Be dangerous for good.

Welcome to the Ruined life!

THE RUINED CONFESSION

Jesus,

I am answering the call of The Ruined Life.

I have been ruined for normal and will not ever be satisfied off of it.

I refuse to go back to who I used to be.

My new normal is holy living, righteous thinking, and grace-filled love.

My life is now Yours, and I humbly ask You for Your love, grace, and guidance to increase my inner anointing.

I surrender my gifts, skills, and talents to You. I will never look to them to validate me. I will celebrate what You do with them because they are Yours.

I declare my spiritual hunger to increase, and I commit to take spiritual responsibility for myself.

I declare I am one who will go when You call—knowing You can move anywhere, anytime, and with anyone.

I declare I am dangerous for good because I carry fearless courage.

I make this declaration in Your name.

Amen.

_____   _____

Signature   Date

APPENDIX
SALVATION: RUINED FOR NORMAL

"If you openly declare that Jesus is Lord and believe in your heart that God raised him from the dead, you will be saved. For it is by believing in your heart that you are made right with God, and it is by openly declaring your faith that you are saved" (Romans 10:9, 10).

God's greatest desire is to love you. When you're in love with someone, you will do things you wouldn't do for other people. Losing sleep to late night phone calls, or spending extra money on a "for no special reason" gift, just to say I love you, are just a few of the things I did to show my wife how special she was for me.

Jesus eclipses us all when He demonstrated His love for us by sacrificing Himself so that He could have uninterrupted relationship with us. This is the part that always gets me. He did all of that with no guarantees that I would give my heart to Him. He did it to show us that He loved us, no matter what condition we meet Him in. In our shame, weakness, and desperation, He met us at our worst, while only focusing on our best. We truly love Him because He loved us first!

Through His death and resurrection, Jesus paid the requirements for our sin, so that we could have a fulfilled life now and on the other side of eternity. This is His gift to us, and to receive this priceless gift, you must first acknowledge your sin is separating you from Him and repent.

Repent means to return. Acts 3:19 says to, "Repent therefore and be converted, that your sins may be blotted out." Sin with all its habits and desires make us slaves to our addictions, issues, and broken patterns. You can't seem to say no or change for the better because you need the love and power Jesus offers you to break the hold of sin and be completely His. Being totally His means you give your life to His Lordship—He becomes the supreme authority and source in your life. When this happens you become ruined for the better. Sin's grip is broken, and you begin to experience life the way God intended you to.

God is asking you to return to Him. If you'd like to make Jesus your Lord and Savior, pray these words:

Jesus,
I ask You to forgive me of my sin. I recognize You were beaten, falsely accused, and put to death for my sin. My sin left me broken, tormented, and empty inside. Thank You for loving me at my worst. I believe You died for my sin, rose again three days later, and You are alive today. Jesus, I confess You as my Lord and Savior. Come into my life and change me into a child of God. I declare I am separated from sin from this day forward and by Your grace I will live for You. Thank You for Your mercy. My life is completely Yours and because of this I will never be ashamed. Amen.

Welcome to the family of God! I encourage you to share what you have just prayed with another Christian immediately. It's also crucial you join a Bible-believing and life-giving church, so you can continue to grow in your new freedom that is found in Jesus. You have just started the journey of being ruined for the better for the rest of your life. I declare you will grow in hunger, revelation, and the grace of almighty God!

KINGDOM IDENTITY

There are two questions people spend their lives trying to answer, "Who am I?" and "What is my purpose?" This world is full of opportunities & choices, and if we don't know our identity and destiny we could end up in a career, relationship, or situation we're not built for. In Kingdom Identity, you'll learn that knowing "what" you're called to is knowing "who" you're called to. But before you know "who" you're called to, you need to know who YOU are. Kingdom Identity will establish unshakeable identity and bring you to your destiny training. It will reveal the inheritance of being "in Christ", it will help you understand the process of lifelong change and transformation, and help develop your God-given identity that will lead you to your destiny track. Get ready as Pastor Chris passionately shares these insights that will give you endurance and clarity to live the life you were designed to live! **Curriculum includes 8 sessions on DVD set & a workbook.**

FIN ISH ER

FINISHER will blow the dust of discouragement, partial obedience, and bad timing off the dreams & assignments of God on your life. This book speaks to everyone who has ever struggled to find the courage to complete everything from marriages, to business plans, to following the call of God on your life, to taking stands for righteousness. It exposes the lies and patterns that try to kill dreamers and paralyze the risk takers from emerging into their God given destiny. We are living in a crucial moment in history and it is vital to let ruthless hope & determination, carry us to finish what He has called us to do. A prophetic call is thundering right now to live from heavens perspective, run with divine focus, & transform society. No more living with regrets & excuses, this book will develop a holy discomfort to FINISH exactly how you started.